APOSTLES IN ENGLAND

Apostles in England

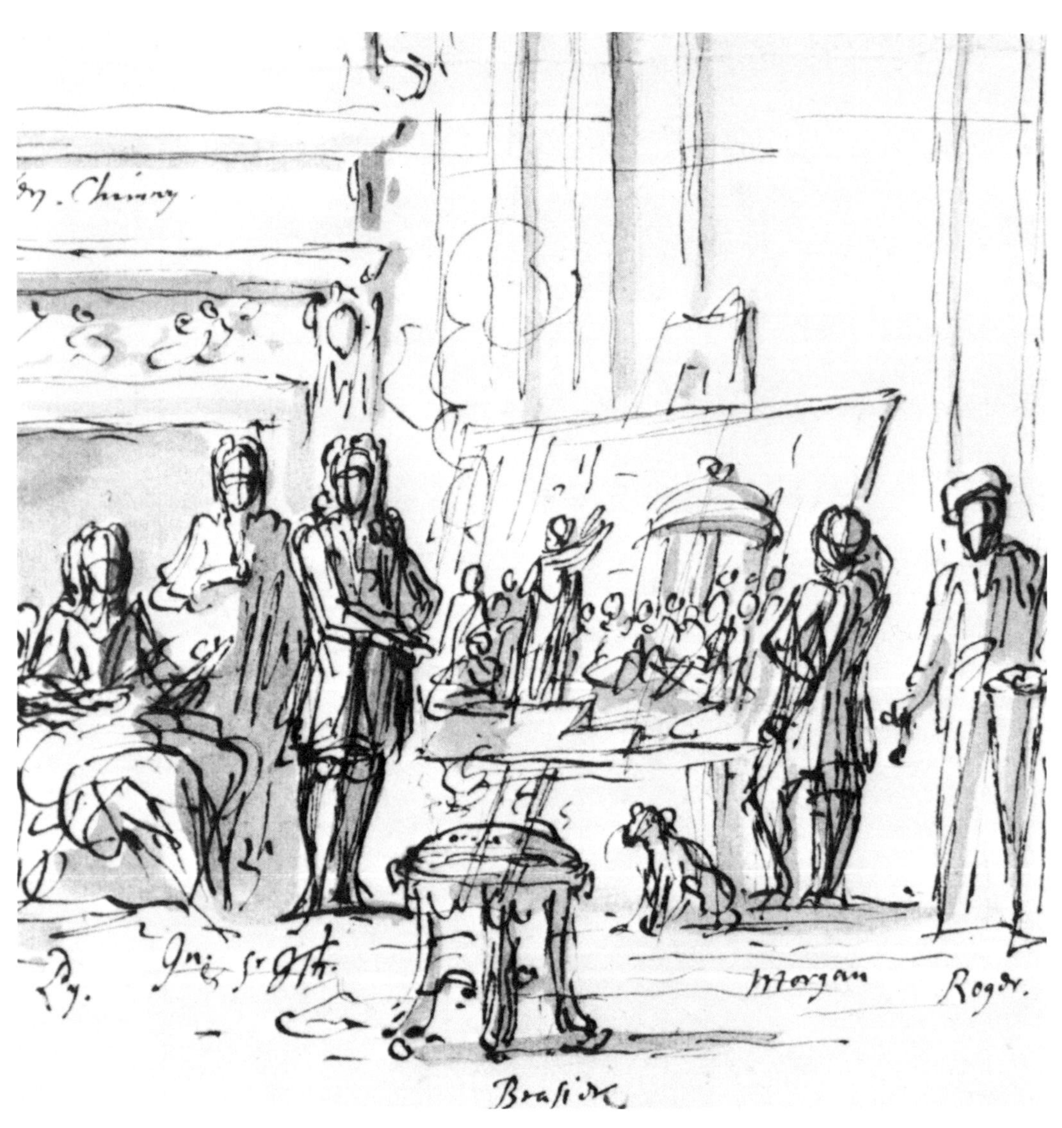

Sir James Thornhill & the Legacy of Raphael's Tapestry Cartoons

by ARLINE MEYER

MIRIAM & IRA D. WALLACH ART GALLERY
COLUMBIA UNIVERSITY IN THE CITY OF NEW YORK

This publication is issued in conjunction with the exhibition *Apostles in England: Sir James Thornhill and the Legacy of Raphael's Tapestry Cartoons* held at the Miriam and Ira D. Wallach Art Gallery, Columbia University in the City of New York, 15 October to 21 December 1996.

The exhibition and the catalogue are made possible through the generosity of the National Endowment for the Arts, the Central-National Gottesman Foundation, and Dr. Lee M. Edwards.

Published by the Miriam and Ira D. Wallach Art Gallery, Columbia University in the City of New York

Library of Congress Catalog Card Number 96–061308
ISBN 1–884919–02–2

Distributed by the University of Washington Press

Frontispiece: detail of figure 25 (cat. 39).

TABLE OF CONTENTS

PREFACE

SINCE 1959, a feature of the premises in Schermerhorn Hall occupied by Columbia University's Department of Art History and Archaeology has been a group of large painted copies of the celebrated Tapestry Cartoons of Raphael. The original Cartoons have been the property of the English Crown since the early seventeenth century, and since 1865 they have been on public view in the Victoria and Albert Museum in London. Our copies have been seen—if not always noticed—by every student of art history at Columbia and are perhaps affectionately remembered by some graduates as familiar parts of the landscape, but they have received no serious attention prior to the present exhibition. Despite the considerable art-historical interest of the copies in their own right—as well as the seminal place of Raphael's compositions in the history of western art—generations of scholars have chosen to look past the paintings on our walls rather than at them, to look at a slide projected on a screen rather than at a hand-painted version of the same composition hanging in a seminar room in which Raphael is being discussed.

Our preference is due, first of all, to the fact that the copies are copies, not works painted by Raphael himself. Since the advent of photography in the mid-nineteenth century and the beginning of the mechanical reproduction of works of art, painted, drawn, and engraved copies, like plaster casts of classical sculptures, have lost their once important role as a primary means of access to admired original works of art; and they have lost their status as respectable sources of aesthetic enjoyment in themselves. We also tend to distrust them, placing greater faith in the accuracy and reliability of purportedly impersonal photographic reproductions. Yet, in the postmodern nineteen-nineties, art historians are often as interested in the afterlife of a work of art as in the work itself, in its reception by different audiences over the years, and in the analysis of differing responses to the work as shaped by history and those responses' role in turn in helping to shape history. Needless to say, copies constitute a visible part of that afterlife. This exhibition also takes place at a time when appropriation as practiced by artists such as Mike Bidlo and Sherrie Levine commands considerable critical attention and respect. Our copies, created as part of a three-year campaign in which the artist James Thornhill made no fewer than three sets of copies of the Cartoons, must be deemed products of one of the most ambitious and remarkable exercises in appropriation in post-Renaissance art.

Furthermore, as indicated by the words that we always employ when referring to the "Tapestry Cartoons," these compositions were created not to be displayed as original works, but for the sake of being copied. The sixteenth-century public that saw Raphael's original paintings consisted only of a handful of Flemish weavers, who promptly cut them into strips as part of their working procedure. Any of the many sets of tapestries woven after the Cartoons in the sixteenth and seventeenth centuries—including a set now belonging to the Cathedral of Saint John the Divine, some six blocks down Amsterdam Avenue from the Wallach Art Gallery—offers a closer approximation of the finished works envisioned by Raphael and his patron Pope Leo X than do the Cartoons themselves. Before the middle years of the nineteenth century, when the Cartoons entered a public museum and were first reproduced photographically, the fame of Raphael's compositions and their great impact upon subsequent artists was due virtually entirely to copies, whether woven, painted, or engraved.

That said, we are still right in most instances to trust our slides in preference to the copies. Columbia's seven paintings were produced far from Italy and more than two centuries after the death of Raphael. However faithfully Thornhill, the copyist, may have intended to reproduce Raphael, he inevitably saw what he was copying through his own eighteenth-century English eyes. Thornhill would have been the first to admit that he was not another Raphael, but he was an artist of stature and reputation, responsible for the paintings in the dome of Saint Paul's Cathedral and the magnificent Painted Hall at Greenwich. These are large-scale, indeed huge, late Baroque decorations which belong to a stylistic world remote from the classically disciplined High Renaissance art of Raphael. Thornhill's most ambitious works were intended for domes or high ceilings to be seen only at vast distances. Concern with finer nuances was not a significant component of his art. In his copies of Raphael, while the overall compositions are accurate, in details such as faces he had neither the mentality nor the inclination to replicate the refinements and subtleties of an artist who was one of the greatest draughtsmen who ever lived.

Thornhill was the father-in-law of William Hogarth. In the history of English art, the differences between the two men may seem more noteworthy than their similarities, but, from a longer perspective, we can see that they did have sensibilities as well as interests in common. Hogarth admired the Tapestry Cartoons and at times strove to emulate their compositions, not with complete success (see fig. 57). In Thornhill's copies, while the heads generally possess little of the sensitivity of their Italian Renaissance prototypes, they do seem to show a John Bull bluntness that calls to mind faces and expressions in slightly later paintings by Hogarth. In such details, albeit in ways completely unintended by Thornhill, we are able to discern a distinctively native English art being born.

Some of our attitude toward Thornhill's copies can also be explained by changing feelings about the originals he copied. As demonstrated and discussed in this exhibition and catalogue, for a century or so after Thornhill copied them no works of art commanded greater respect or had a more pervasive influence on the practice of painting than

Raphael's Tapestry Cartoons.[1] That influence, whether felt directly by artists in England such as Thornhill, who had the opportunity to study the original Cartoons, or transmitted elsewhere at one remove by artists themselves profoundly influenced by the Cartoons such as Poussin, became the cornerstone of academic notions of what art should be and remained so until the academy and academic art started to become anathema to progressive younger artists and critics.[2] With the rejection of the academy came rejection of Raphael, as evidenced by the name "Pre-Raphaelite Brotherhood" that a group of young English painters gave to their would-be revolutionary organization founded in 1848. Such rejection was not absolute. The Pre-Raphaelites, like the German Nazarenes before them, actually took a lot from Raphael, but from the earlier, sweeter, simpler, more devotional painter of Madonnas rather than the later creator of the more compositionally elaborate and dramatic Cartoons.[3] When the Pre-Raphaelites were censured for the blasphemous name that they had chosen for themselves, they tried to draw a distinction between the artist Raphael, for whom they claimed they intended no disrespect, and later "Raphaelite" art, created by mindless imitators, who by 1848 had become wholly and hopelessly conventional.[4] Thornhill's copies, other copies and engravings represented in this exhibition, and the uses to which this material was put, which are discussed by Professor Meyer in the following pages, all served to create an initially fruitful but eventually stifling academicism that by the middle of the nineteenth century progressive artists everywhere were driven to reject. Although the main enemy was what came after Raphael, the dependence of so much academic art upon the Cartoons led to some far-from-respectful dismissals of those previously universally respected works. For John Ruskin, the critical champion of the Pre-Raphaelite Brotherhood, the Cartoons, which he was taken to see as a boy, "began to take the aspect of mild nightmare and nuisance which they have ever since retained."[5]

We are heirs to the revolutions of the nineteenth century and the attitudes they engendered. Nevertheless, by now those revolutions belong to a past from which we are separated by a cultural gulf almost as great as the one created by the nearly five-hundred years that lie between us and Raphael. We can look at Raphael, if we choose, without thinking too much about all that may have transpired between the early sixteenth and the late twentieth centuries, and to understand Raphael we should try to. But, for art historians, the eighteenth-

1. "The seven cartoons . . . have been called 'the Parthenon sculptures of modern art' and certainly they surpass the great Vatican frescoes in fame and the extent of their influence. They can be used as models for compositions with a limited number of figures and they have been widely diffused in woodcut and engraved reproductions. They were a thesaurus of forms expressing all human emotions and Raphael's fame as a draughtsman is mainly based on these achievements." Heinrich Wölfflin, *Classic Art,* 1899, tr. P. and L. Murray, 1948, 108.

2. For an intriguing demonstration of the Cartoons' continuing influence upon the academic curriculum, see the reproductions of paintings that won the French Prix de Rome between 1797 and 1863 in Philippe Grunchec, *The Grand Prix de Rome: Paintings from the Ecole des Beaux-Arts 1797–1863,* exh. cat., International Exhibitions Foundation, 1984–85.

3. See, for example, M. Warner, "The Pre-Raphaelites and the National Gallery," in *The Pre-Raphaelites in Context,* M. Warner et al., Henry E. Huntington Library and Art Gallery, San Marino, CA, 1992, 5.

4. See particularly the two letters and the pamphlet written in defense of the Pre-Raphaelites by John Ruskin in 1851 in *The Works of John Ruskin,* ed. E. T. Cook and A. Wedderburn, 39 vols., 1903–12, 12:319–27, 339–93.

5. In *Praeterita,* ibid., 35:247.

century obsession with the Cartoons is fascinating to observe and is important to study because of the Cartoons' immense significance for developments, both good and bad, in the art of the eighteenth and nineteenth centuries. The works in this exhibition are part of history and of art history, enriched by and enriching our understanding of the past and the art of the past, including some of the greatest art in a tradition that still for us at the end of the twentieth century, as for Thornhill and his contemporaries at the beginning of the eighteenth, constitutes a vital and central part of our cultural heritage.

The welcome idea of taking a closer look at our copies of the Cartoons and at their place in the history of art was proposed to us by Professor Arline Meyer of Ohio State University, who has subsequently borne the responsibility of organizing this exhibition and writing its catalogue. As a former student and colleague at Columbia who has spent many an hour in the company of these paintings, and as the author of several studies of English art of the first half of the eighteenth century, she has brought to the project an ideal mix of affectionate familiarity with the works themselves and informed awareness of their place in a larger historical context. We at Columbia are grateful to Professor Meyer for enriching our lives by giving us new eyes to see what has been here waiting to be seen.

The exhibition has been made possible in part by a grant from the National Endowment for the Arts and by a gift from Dr. Lee M. Edwards. Publication of the catalogue has been assisted by a subvention from the Wallach Art Gallery Publication Fund, established by the Central National–Gottesman Foundation.

Allen Staley
Chairman, Department of Art History and Archaeology

ACKNOWLEDGMENTS

TO THE MANY curators, librarians, colleagues, and friends whose interest in the subject of Raphael in eighteenth-century England and whose generosity and expertise have contributed so substantially to the exhibition and to the publication of this catalogue, I appreciatively offer thanks.

I am especially indebted to several sponsoring institutions: the Miriam and Ira D. Wallach Art Gallery for providing the perfect venue; the College of the Arts and the History of Art Department at the Ohio State University for two grants and a quarter-term leave that supported my research; the American Philosophical Society for a travel grant to London; and the National Endowment of the Arts for a special-exhibitions grant.

To all the lenders who are listed on page xiii I want to offer my thanks for making this exhibition possible. Invaluable assistance was also provided by many libraries and museums whose participation may not be visible on the walls but who nonetheless are, thanks to their helpful staffs and valuable holdings, partners in this exhibition: Bodleian Library, British Museum, Pierpont Morgan Library, Tate Gallery, Rijksmuseum, Royal Academy, Saint Paul's Cathedral Library, and the Print and Drawing Collection of Her Majesty the Queen at Windsor Castle.

For assistance in the preparation of this essay during its various early stages, Judy Sund (foremost among friends and colleagues) deserves particular thanks for her careful reading of the manuscript and her many judicious suggestions; my colleagues at Ohio State, Barbara Haeger and Ruth Melville, provided much appreciated editorial assistance. Allen Staley's critical scrutiny of the text led to marked improvements in the final version.

Among those who have offered me assistance in many different ways, I especially want to thank Brian Allen, Georgia Barnhill, Catherine Bindman, Joy Gould Boyum, Ellen Chirlstein, Martin Clayton, David Combs, John Cornforth, David Cunningham, Robert Dance, William Drummond, Marlene Edelheit, Elizabeth Einberg, Sharon Fermor, Burton Fredericksen, Angela Giral, Janice Glowski, Eileen Harris, John Harris, Jonathan Harris, Rica Jones, Martin Krause, Gwydwr Leitch, Carol Lewine, Shelly Langdale, Alisa Luxemberg, Elizabeth Miller, Brian D. Mitchell, Patrick Noon, Ellen G. d'Oench, Janet Parks, Bruce Robertson, Nicholas Savage, Charles Sebag-Montefiore, Janet Skidmore, Roger Stoddard, Joan H. Sussler, Marilyn Symmes, Brian Tuppen, Neil Turtell, Helen

Valentine, Roberta Waddell, Michael Webb, David Weinglass, Richard Wendorf, and Joseph Wisdom.

This project has come to pass because of the enthusiastic response, from the time that I submitted the proposal, from Allen Staley, chairman of the department, and Sarah Elliston Weiner, director of the gallery. Professionally, I could not have had better assistance and, from a purely personal perspective, I could not have enjoyed it more. I especially want to thank Professor Staley for the guidance and assistance he has so unstintingly given, and Sarah Weiner for handling all aspects of publishing this catalogue and mounting the exhibition with the calm of a saint. Thanks also to members of the gallery staff: Jonathan Munk, Toni Simon, and Larry Soucy. A further accolade goes to Jerry Kelly for the finesse of his catalogue design and the pleasure of working with him.

As a final note, I thank my closest supporters, my daughter, Claudia, whom I forgive for editing the *Ecology Law Quarterly* rather than my text, and Valentine Russell for his supportive encouragement of my work.

As an alumna of the department I confess to having been as guilty as any of having ignored these pictures for so long; I am glad for this opportunity to make amends.

Arline Meyer
Curator of the exhibition

LENDERS TO THE EXHIBITION

Grateful acknowledgment is extended to the following for their generosity in making this exhibition possible:

American Antiquarian Society, Worcester, Massachusetts

Columbia University in the City of New York
  Avery Architectural and Fine Arts Library
  Butler Library

Museum of Fine Arts, Boston

Burghley House Collection

The Cathedral Church of St. John the Divine, New York

Cooper-Hewitt, National Design Museum, Smithsonian Institution

Cornell University Library

Guildhall Library, Corporation of London

The Metropolitan Museum of Art

Miriam and Ira D. Wallach Division of Art, Prints and Photographs, The New York Public Library, Astor, Lenox and Tilden Foundations

Victoria and Albert Museum, London

National Gallery of Art Library, Washington, D.C.

The Lewis Walpole Library, Yale University

Yale Center for British Art

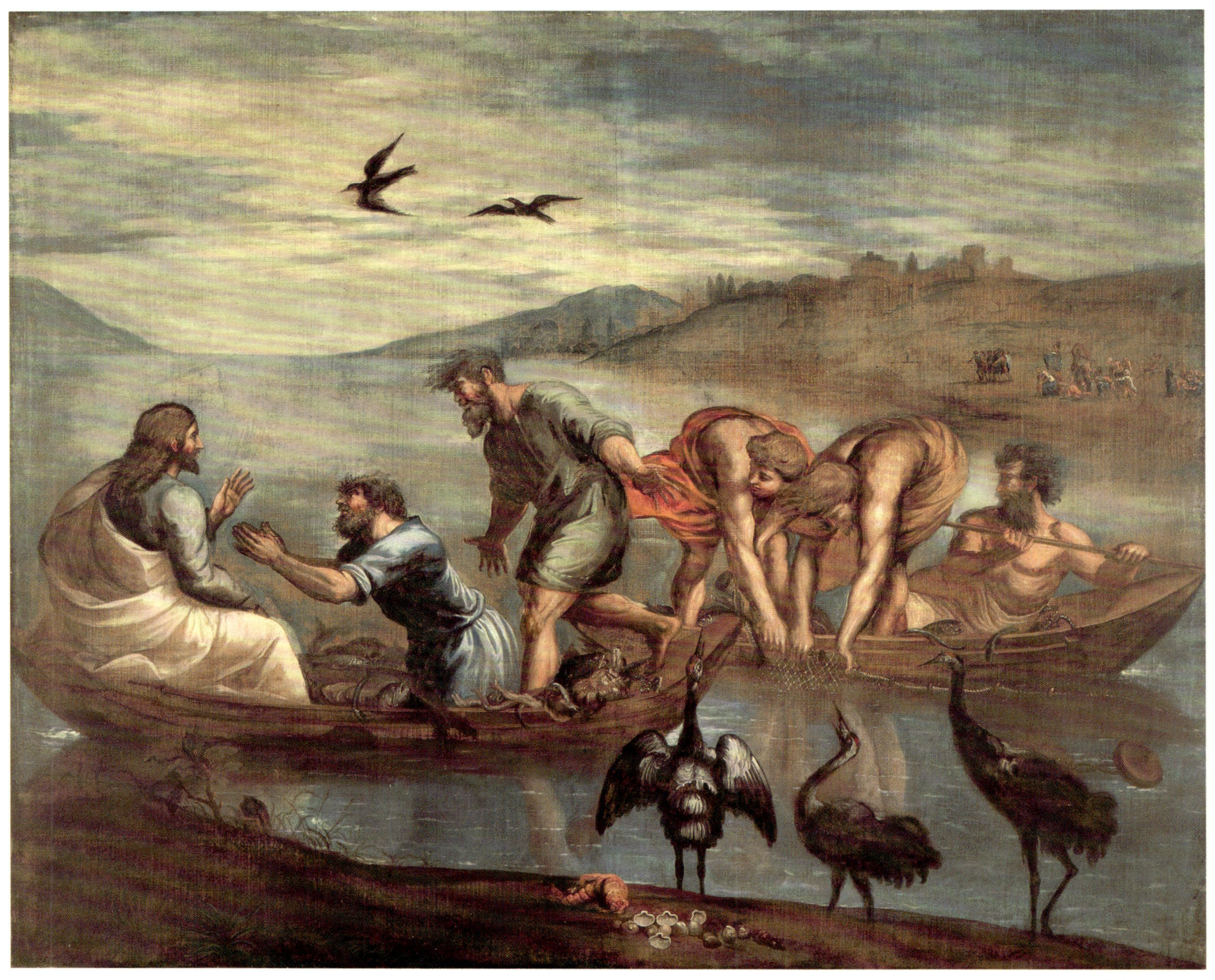

FIG. 1 James Thornhill (after Raphael), *The Miraculous Draught of Fishes*, ca.1729–31 (*cat. 32*)

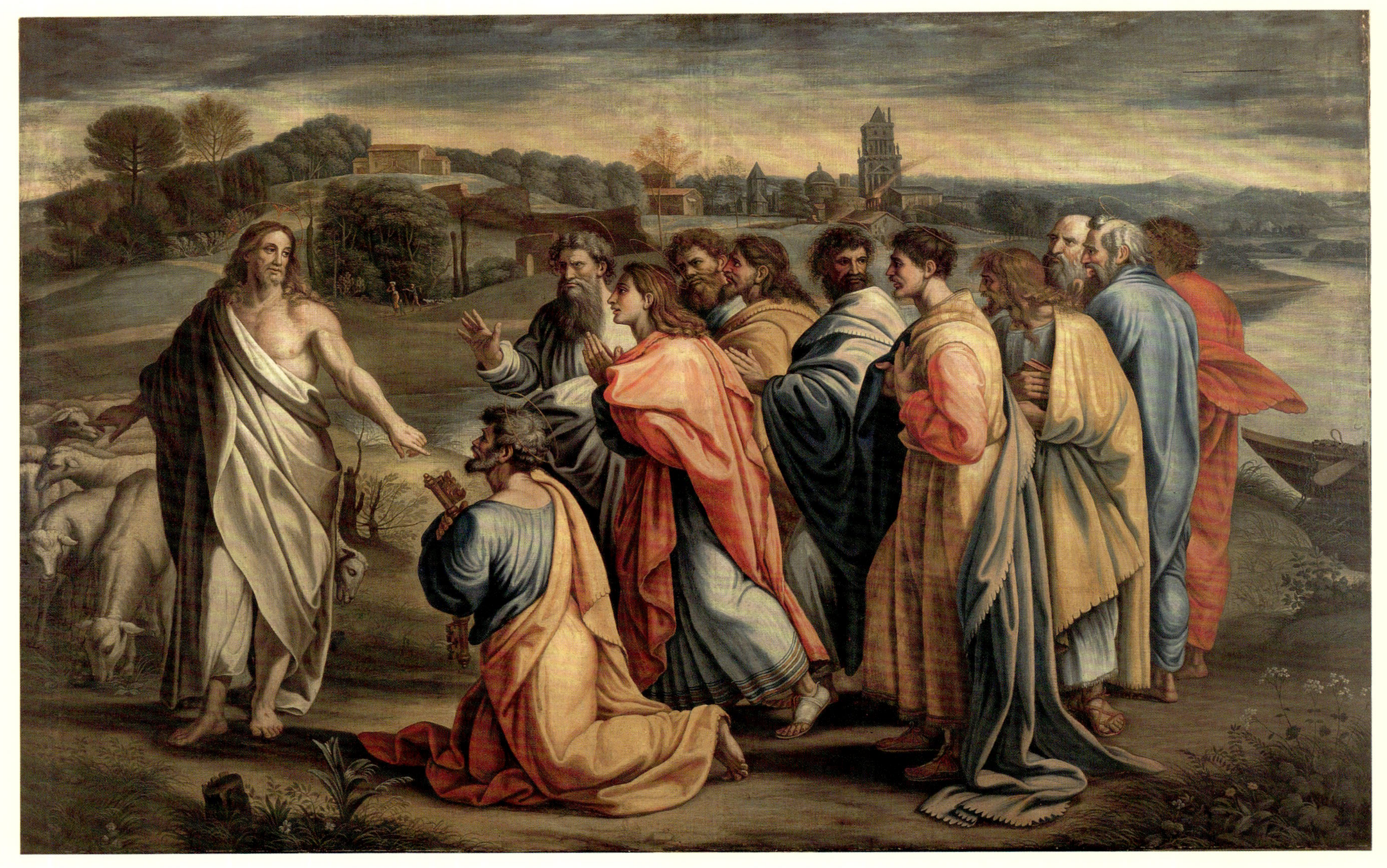

FIG. 2 James Thornhill (after Raphael), *Christ's Charge to Peter*, ca.1729–31 (*cat. 33*)

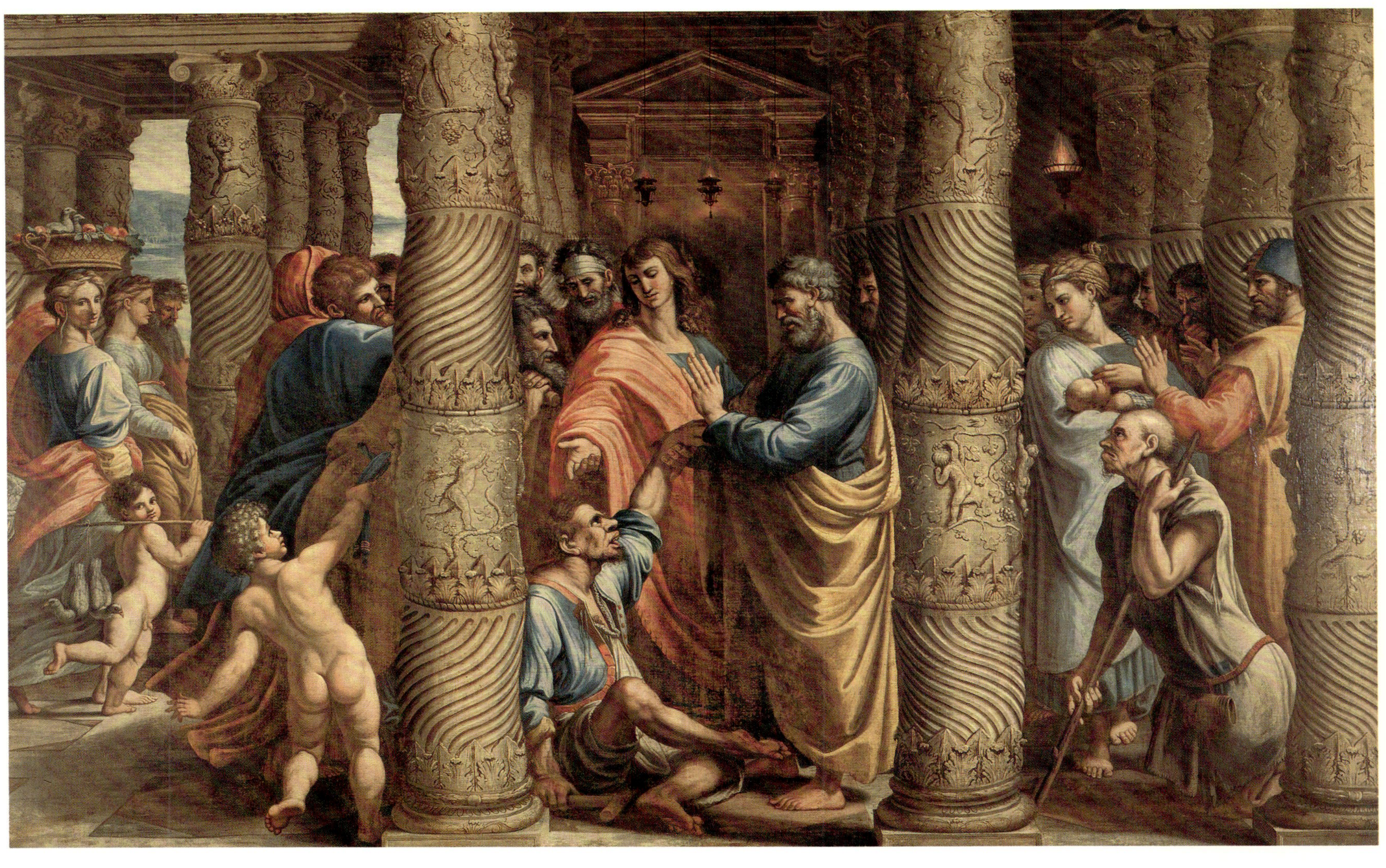

FIG. 3 James Thornhill (after Raphael), *The Lame Man Healed*, ca.1729–31 (*cat. 34*)

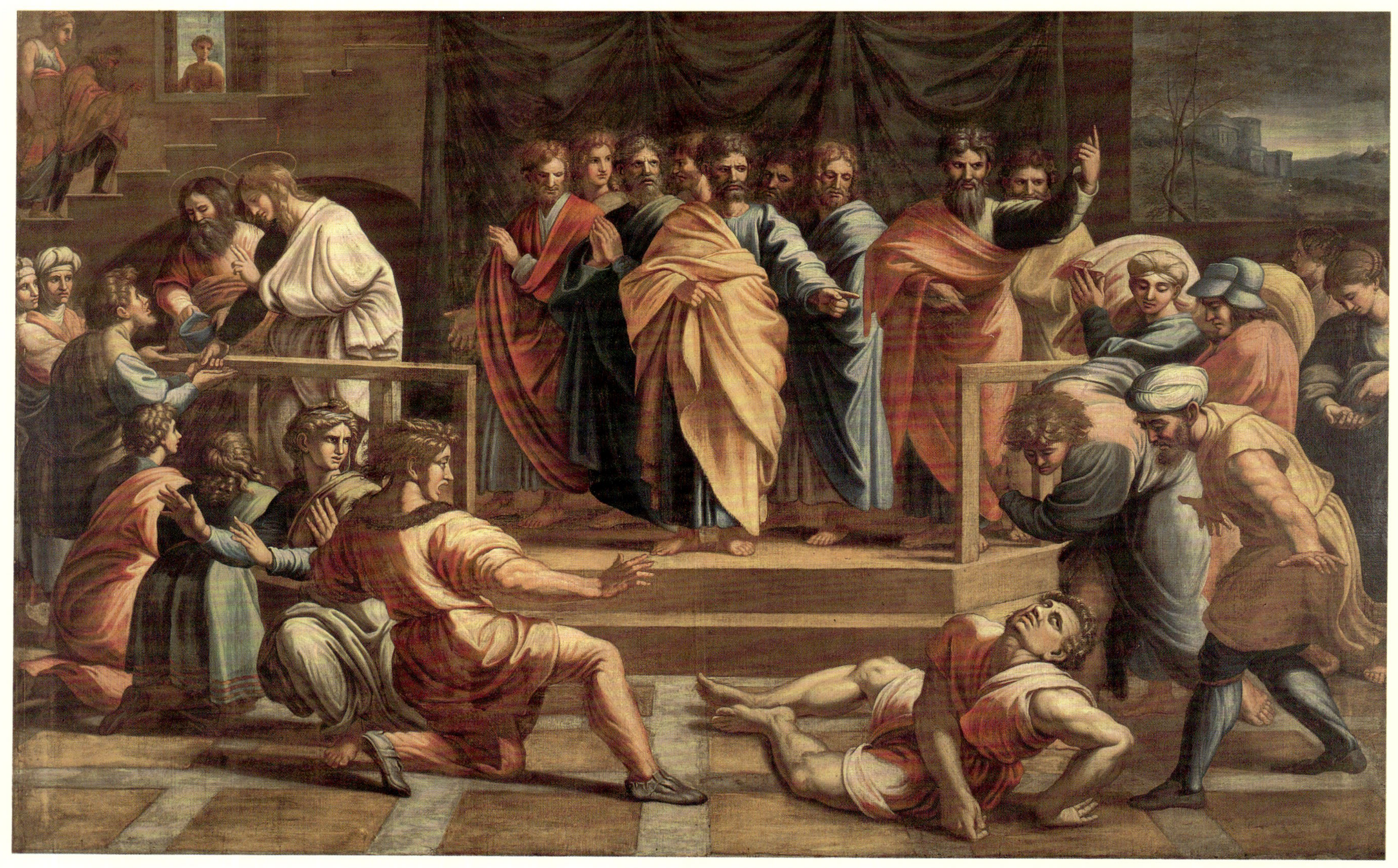

FIG. 4 James Thornhill (after Raphael), *The Death of Ananias*, ca.1729–31 (*cat. 35*)

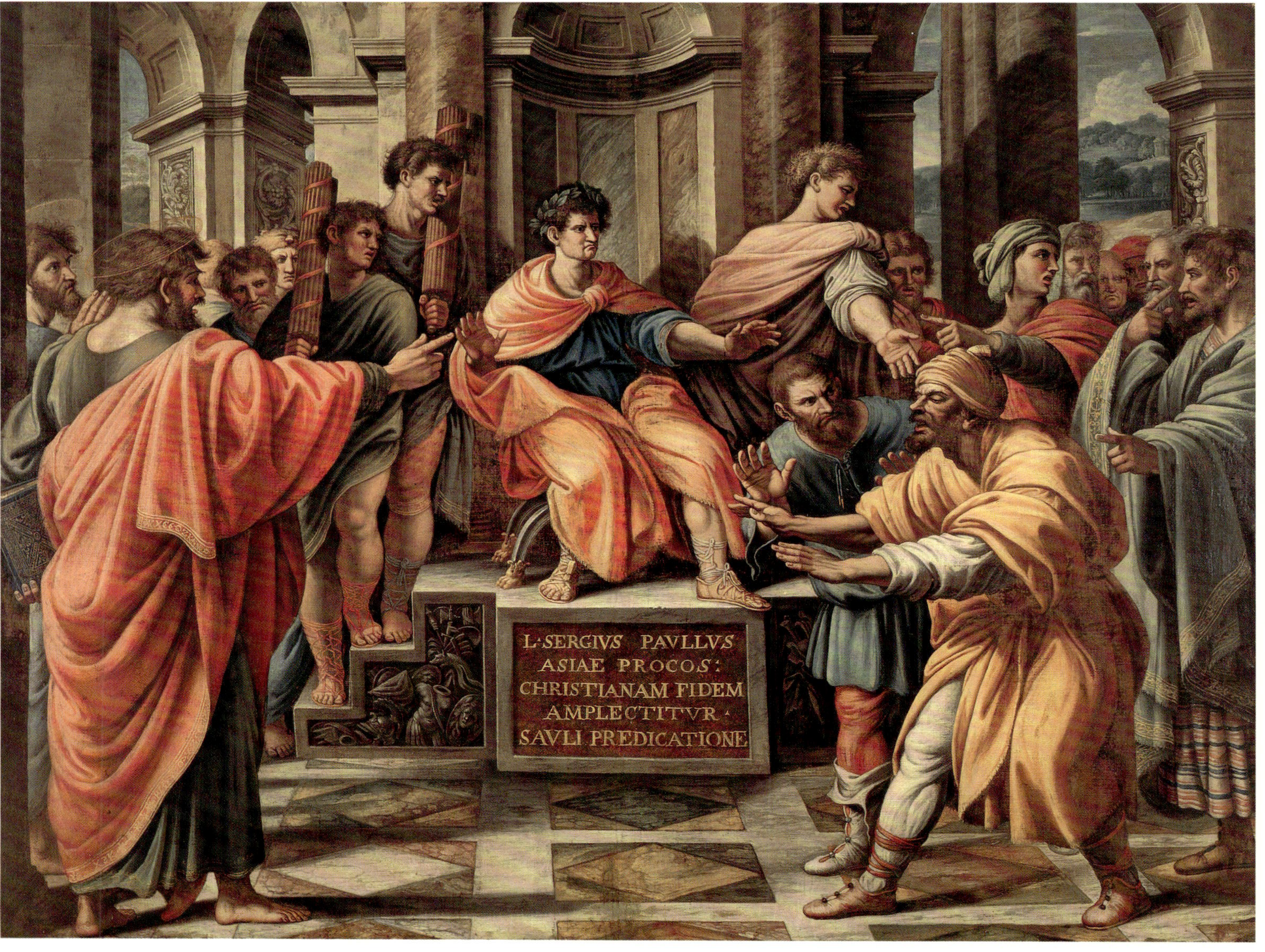

FIG. 5 James Thornhill (after Raphael), *Elymas the Sorcerer Struck with Blindness*, ca.1729–31 (*cat. 36*)

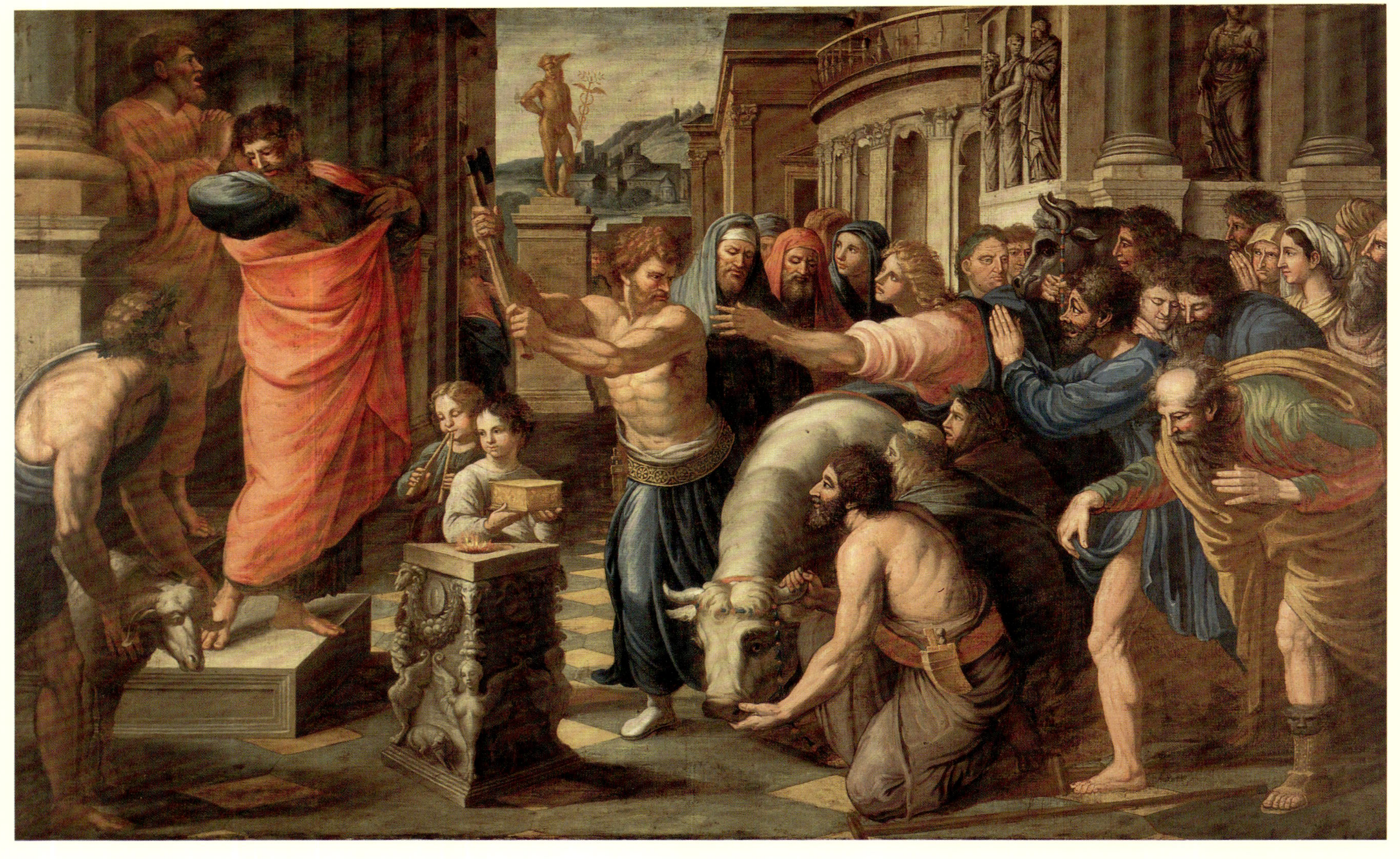

FIG. 6 James Thornhill (after Raphael), *Paul and Barnabas at Lystra*, ca.1729–31 (*cat. 37*)

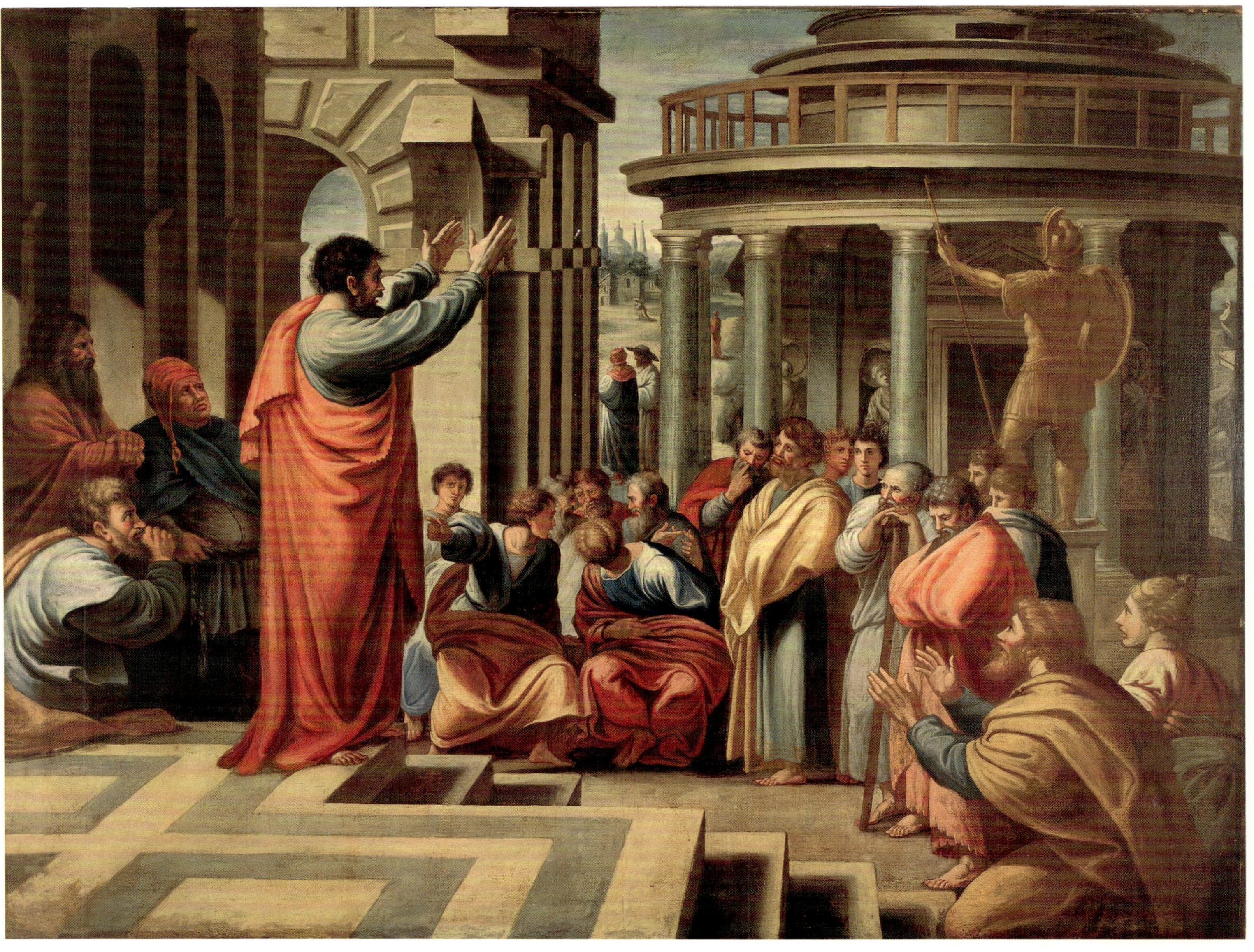

FIG. 7 James Thornhill (after Raphael), *Paul Preaching at Athens*, ca.1729–31 (*cat. 38*)

INTRODUCTORY REMARK TO "DESCRIPTION OF THE CARTOONS OF RAPHAEL URBIN"

The following description of Raphael's Tapestry Cartoons was first published by John Boydell in 1759 in The School of Raphael, *a book of practical academic instruction that promoted the Cartoons as a primary course of study for artists. He reissued the text in 1764 under the new title* A Description of the Cartoons of Raphael Urbin, in the Queen's Palace, *the year after the Cartoons were moved from Hampton Court to Buckingham Palace.*[1] *Assuming that a printed explanation would be welcomed by the many who could now see these celebrated works at their new location, Boydell took the opportunity to accommodate the public's interest as well as his own.*

This text–which served as an aesthetic tutor to eighteenth-century viewers–now serves as our guide to the artistic preoccupations of that original audience. The author provides the biblical source and a detailed account of the salient features of each of the seven subjects illustrated and notes where Raphael's invention, design, expression, variety, and decorum merit special comment.

1. The Cartoons hung at Hampton Court from 1699 to 1763. Fourteen years later, in the course of a speech to Parliament in 1777 (in which he proposed establishing a national gallery), John Wilkes reproved George III for having moved the Cartoons, claiming that "at present they are perishing in a late Baronet's smoky house at the end of a great smoky town . . . entirely secluded from the public eye" (Whitley, 1:326–27). In 1787 the Cartoons were moved again, this time to Windsor Castle. They were returned to Hampton Court in 1804, at which point they were reinstalled in a different order than previously (figs. 8 and 9). In 1865 the Cartoons found a permanent home in South Kensington in what would become the Victoria and Albert Museum.

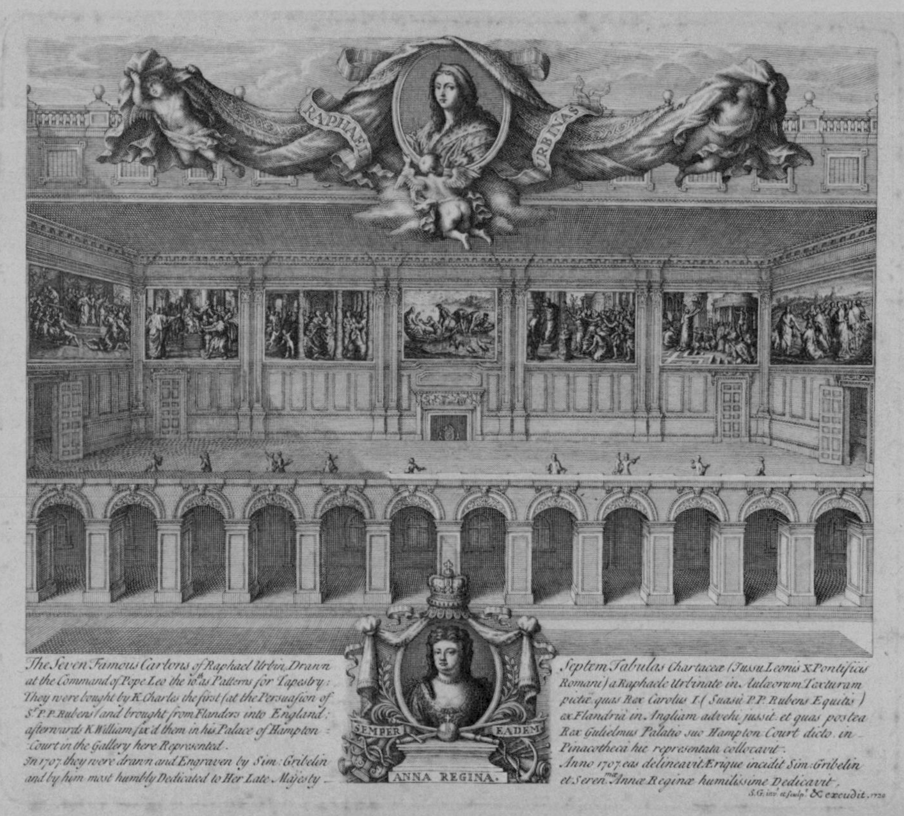

FIG. 8 Simon Gribelin, *View of the Hampton Court Cartoon Gallery*, ca.1720 (*cat. 9*)

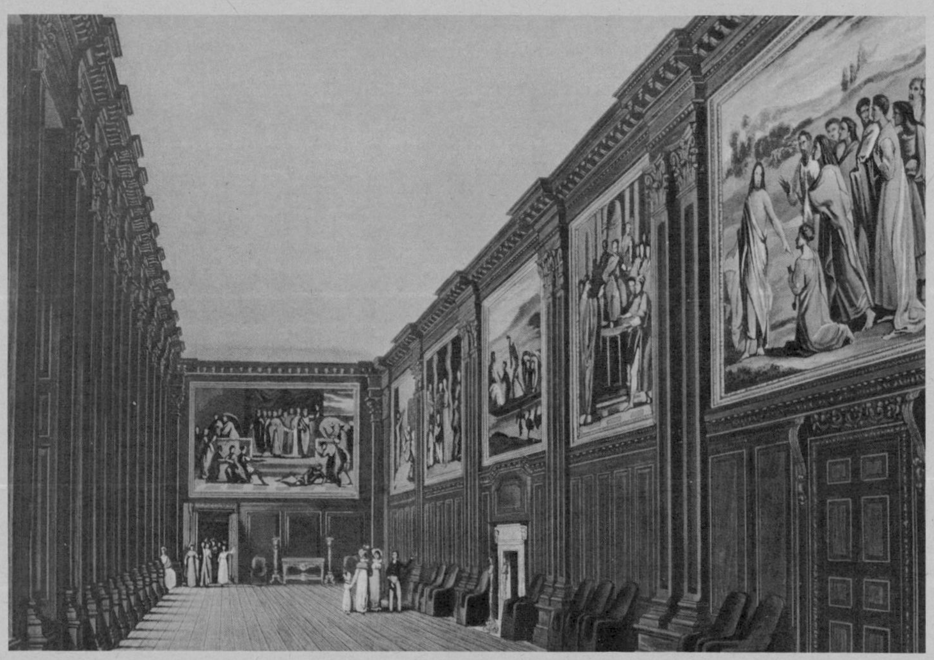

FIG. 9 *View of the Hampton Court Gallery*, detail, in William H. Pyne, *History of the Royal Residences*, vol. 2, 1819 (*cat. 2*)

DESCRIPTION
OF THE
CARTOONS OF RAPHAEL URBIN

When a man enters into that awful Gallery at Hampton Court, (says Mr. [Jonathan] Richardson, in his Essay on the Theory of Painting) he finds himself amongst a sort of people superior to what he has ever seen, and very probably to what those really were. Indeed this is (speaking of grace and greatness) the principal excellence of those wonderful pictures, as it must be allowed to be that part of painting which is preferable to all others. These inimitable pieces are called Cartoons, from their being executed upon paper; and are nothing more than coloured drawings, upon a washed ground previously prepared for that purpose, the shadows of which are made by hatching with the point of a large pencil, and the whole are very highly finished. They were originally intended as patterns for tapestry, and were entirely the work of that great master Raphael Urbin. It is almost impossible to consider these pictures, without supposing that, as the Miraculous Draught of Fishes is the only miracle of our Saviour's to be found among them, it is more than probable, that what this country now happily possesses, is but a part of a most stupenduous work of this great man, and that many more glorious Cartoons of the life and miracles of our Saviour have perished in oblivion; for it can hardly be conceived, that this single subject could particularly engage the attention of Raphael, among many others which would undoubtedly have made better pictures, and been more suitable to his genius; and the Cartoon of Christ's Charge to Peter, and the regular succession of the acts of the Apostle, seem greatly to confirm this opinion. However, as it is an argument that probably will not be contested, and cannot be proved, it can only be lamented, that perhaps some accident, or the premature death of that great master, has deprived the world of an invaluable treasure.

CARTOON 1

THE MIRACULOUS DRAUGHT OF FISHES

And Jesus said unto Simon, Fear not, from henceforth thou shalt catch men.—LUKE V. 10

THIS WAS an amazing event; but as the principal persons were few, and half of them necessarily engaged in the management of their nets, the historical expression is confined to three figures only, which are those of our Saviour, Peter, and James. The principal figure of this picture is Christ, who is pronouncing the words above quoted, in order to remove the apprehension of Peter, who, in a fine posture of supplication, has just uttered these words, "Depart from me, for I am a sinful man, O Lord." Our Saviour's figure and action are perfectly great and graceful; and in his character, divinity, benignity, and tenderness, are expressed in the highest degree. In Peter's countenance, fear, wonder, and solicitude are blended in a most extraordinary manner, and compose a character of expression worthy of Raphael; the figure in the same boat, supposed to be that of James, is also finely imagined and drawn; awe and attention are strongly marked in his face, and he seems, by his action, to have acquiesced in the supplication of Peter, as acknowledging himself unworthy of being the companion of Divinity. The rest of the figures, as has already been said, are chiefly concerned in attending to their employment, which, as they were in another vessel, naturally engrossed their attention; only the nearest of them seems to have caught some part of the conversation, and appears to listen: this last figure, and another, who are pulling up the net, are finely drawn, contrasted, and foreshortened; and the whole figure of the old man in the stern of the boat, who is very attentive to his business, is extremely fine.

The perspective in this Cartoon (in which the point of sight is placed pretty high) occasions the sea to make a fine back ground for the figures, which, from its natural hue, fails not of shewing the colouring of the figures to the utmost advantage. At a great distance, upon the sea-shore, appear several groupes of figures, designed in a masterly manner, the principal of which seems to consist of a number of persons who are employed in the baptism of infants. Nothing need be said to the objection commonly made by small critics to the size of the boats, that having been fully answered by Mr. Richardson; who has also mentioned the effect of the sea-fowl, which are artfully and judiciously placed in the fore ground, and indeed could be very ill spared.

CARTOON II

CHRIST'S CHARGE TO PETER; COMMONLY CALLED THE DELIVERY OF THE KEYS

He said unto him the third time, Simon, son of Jonas, lovest thou me? Peter was grieved because he said unto him the third time, Lovest thou me? And he said unto him, Lord, thou knowest all things, thou knowest that I love thee. Jesus saith unto him, Feed my sheep.—JOHN XXI. 17

THE PRINCIPAL figure in this picture is that of our Saviour, which Mr. Richardson is of opinion has received some injury, and is not at present what Raphael made it. This supposition, it is believed, has never been contradicted; and whoever attentively compares the taste of design in this figure with those of the apostles in the same Cartoon, or that of our Saviour in the Miraculous Draught of Fishes, must be convinced that it falls many degrees short of that great painter. Perhaps, by some who may contend for its being Raphael's, it may be urged, that, like Leonardo da Vinci, in a similar case, he was baffled by the greatness of his own idea: but whichever argument holds good, we must be content to take it as it appears. Mr. Richardson also observes, that the time chosen is the moment of our Lord's having just spoken; and that in consequence of our Saviour's interrogating Peter, "Lovest thou me more than these?" the rest of the apostles were eager to reply to that question, by assuring their Lord, that their love for him was at least equal to Peter's; and this solicitude is finely expressed in every character. The next principal figure is that of Peter, who, according to the history, is represented upon his knees, with the utmost humility attending to and receiving the charge given him by his divine Master. The head is drawn in profile, and the face is entirely in shadow. It may be here observed, that the shadow cast by Peter's body serves admirably to bring the figure of our Saviour forward, and also to keep the principal groupe together. The third principal figure is St. John, whose expression and attitude Mr. Richardson mentions as an improvement upon the story. He says, our Saviour, by commanding Peter to feed his sheep seemed to indicate a preference in favour of that apostle, as has been observed; and that St. John, who was the beloved disciple, may, therefore, be supposed to have been under a particular concern on that account. Accordingly he appears to address himself to our Lord with extreme ardour, as if earnestly endeavouring to convince him of the sincerity of his love. The attention of all the apostles is directed to our Saviour, except one, who seems to press forward: and, by turning his head, which is seen between two profiles, hinders the repetition which would have unavoidably happened if he had been looking the same way. The heads of the apostles are amazingly designed, and full of expression; and their attitudes are finely varied and contrasted. The draperies are noble and well cast; that of our Saviour only appears to be rather heavy, and unsuitable to him at this time, as being after his resurrection. But admitting that this figure has suffered, the injury may, in this particular, be attributed to the alteration of it by some other hand. Mr. Richardson, who had studied the Cartoons observes, that the small piece of drapery in a part of the outermost apostle, is of great consequence to this picture; which, being folded as under his arm, breaks the straight line of an unpleasing mass of light, and gives a more graceful form to the whole: which artifice is also assisted by the boat. Of the same consequence to the principal figure is the flock of sheep placed behind, which helps to break the lines of the drapery, detach the figure from its ground, and illustrate the history.

CARTOON III

THE LAME MAN HEALED; COMMONLY CALLED THE BEAUTIFUL GATE OF THE TEMPLE

Then Peter said, Silver and gold have I none, but such as I have give I thee: in the name of Jesus Christ of Nazareth, rise up and walk.
And he took him by the right hand, and lifted him up, and immediately his feet and ancle bones received strength.—ACTS III. 6, 7

THIS TRULY GREAT composition is divided into three distinct groupes, by means of the magnificent columns which appear in the front of the picture, and are a part of the colonade which supports the roof of the portico. The two apostles Peter and John, the cripple, and four figures, whose heads only are seen, compose the groupe in the centre; one side of the picture is filled with people going to the temple, and its opposite with others coming from it; which disposition Raphael has advantageously employed in contrasting these two subordinate groupes, by opposing the backs of some of the figures to others which are seen in front, and further contrasting these by several which are in profile.

There is not, perhaps, in the world, a picture so thoroughly characterised, or so artfully managed, as this Cartoon. The moment of Peter's having pronounced the words, "In the name of Jesus Christ of Nazareth, rise up and walk," is the time chosen by Raphael; and is the instant when the lame man finds himself suddenly enabled to rise; when the muscles of his limbs, released from the contraction which till now withheld and deprived him of their use, are expanding, and an extraordinary impulse urges him to the exertion of their hitherto useless functions; all which is most amazingly conceived and expressed. At this period, those who were apprized of something extraordinary which was then transacting, are endeavouring to thrust forward on the side of the picture where the cripple is placed; and these, with a woman and boy who are hastily passing on to the temple, together with the inimitable boy in the front of the picture, who is eagerly pulling back one of the figures, remarkably characterize the principal subject of the cartoon, which is that of the agents of Divine Power giving strength and agility to the torpid limbs of a man who was born lame. Wonder and amazement are finely expressed in the characters of the spectators; and on the side of the picture next to Peter, who with great dignity has conferred the divine gift, every thing is still, but expressing silent amazement. Thus in the parts where dignity should be preserved, all is quiet; and where strength and activity are given every thing is in motion.

The character of the cripple is finely imagined; it is perfectly that of a mean person; and the expression of joy and gratitude which appears in it, is finely balanced by a mixture of doubt and astonishment; and he seems scarcely to believe the reality of the blessing he is receiving. The character of Peter is devout and majestic; and that of John is full of divinity, and superlatively graceful; he is represented with the utmost pity and affability, concurring with Peter in this act of true piety and charity. The rest of the heads in the same groupe are finely invented and drawn, particularly that of the old man leaning upon his crutch, and of him who is looking over John's shoulder.

It is remarkable, that the same airs of the head, which Raphael has given to the two apostles, are nearly the same with those of the man and woman on that side of the picture; and the action of Peter's arm is repeated in the same man with a very little variation. He has also introduced another cripple into this groupe whose character is not altogether unlike that of him who is healed; but the expression is of another kind, and shews a malevolence and disinclination to believe the truth of this miracle; which seems to be one reason why he was placed behind the apostle, as a situation most properly adapted to one of his way of thinking; but this figure is of prodigious use, and is moreover a fine contrast to the other; and the repetition in the rest is so judiciously managed, that it has no ill effect; but of this groupe particular notice will be taken in speaking of the by-works or ornaments of this Cartoon.

There is a wonderful expression of malignity in the character of the man who presses his lips with his finger, in the same groupe. The woman with the child in her arms has a character full of expression, is exquisitely designed, and perfectly great and graceful. The fine boy in the fore part of the picture, who being unconcerned is eager to be going, and pulls the man's garment, is a fine contrast to the figure of the cripple; and at the same time breaks a mass of shadow, which would otherwise have had a very disagreeable effect. This boy is also contrasted by another, who is led along hastily by a woman with a basket upon her head; and these, as has already been observed, give motion to that side of the picture. The drapery upon this woman's arm is artfully swelled and folded towards the elbow, and breaks the straitness which would have appeared from her action, and could not but have offended the eye. It will now be proper to speak of the ornaments, and other accidental decorations, which are usually called bye works.

The principal of these are the columns, which with regard to the picture, are the finest that could possibly be imagined, and in themselves are a proof of the amazing genius of Raphael. The effect of the *waving line*, as an ornament, is perhaps nowhere made use of to such advantage, nor better proves its gracefulness. To confirm this assertion, let one any substitute in their stead, or ideally substitute the Ionic or Corinthian, or any other order; and let it be enriched with flutings, and all the decorations that can possibly be given to those orders, and then compare it with Raphael's. What an astonishing alteration must ensue! How cutting, how disagreeably heavy will the innovation appear! and how very considerably must the picture suffer by the change! Besides, as the columns were arbitrary, and the painter had once deviated from the established rules, he was at liberty to do what he pleased; and therefore Raphael has apparently made use of this licence for the purpose following: It was doubtless necessary that the principal groupe should not only possess the center of the picture, but occupy more space than the others, in order to maintain its character of distinction from the subordinate ones: in consequence of which, Raphael has made the intercolumniation greater between the first and second column, than between the second and third, a part of which is cut off by the side of the picture. This being allowed, it will not be difficult to give what is apprehended will be thought a sufficient reason for the repetitions before mentioned; and why the same number of figures, nearly in the same attitudes, the cripple excepted, were introduced into this groupe. It is certain, that if this part of the picture had been otherwise managed than it is, by too great a variation in the attitudes from those of the principal groupe, the inequality of the intercolumniation would have been more apparent; and consequently every common observer would have taken the liberty of condemning it as an oversight in Raphael. The great artifice, therefore, is concealed in the similitude of the figures which compose these groupes. The same number are employed in both. In the principal groupe, the whole figure of the cripple is seen; in the other the body is large, but being upon his knees, his legs are hid by the column, and the space occupied by his hand and arm, which rests upon a staff, is by no means equivalent to the room gained by the disappearing of his legs; and yet this staff and limb seem to fill up the space. The distance from the knees of the cripple to the column, is greater than that between the feet of the lame man and the same column; and both being near the ground-line or front of the picture, cause a great deception. The woman with the child in her arms is similar to John; but she is placed much nearer the column. John's arm is moderately extended, and his hand appears directly over the cripple's head; the woman's arm is employed in holding the child, and consequently does not appear; and a light, well-folded piece of drapery supplies the place, and forms a mass which receives the shadowed parts of the cripple's head and body. The man is in an attitude similar to that of Peter; but the column is placed so as to be partly hid by his hand, by which he expresses his astonishment, falls exactly in the centre between the two columns, as does that of Peter in the principal groupe: but lest this should be too remarkable, the hand of the woman is seen close by it, naturally and gracefully applied to her breast; and this, with the infant's head, makes a sufficient variation, and does not in the least destroy the principal intention. It being absolutely necessary to introduce the whole arm of the figure of the man, and the hand being to be placed in the centre, the arm is unavoidably required to be bent rather more than that of Peter; but this was not a sufficient variation, and therefore a kind of short open sleeve, which reaches about half way down to the elbow, was added; and this also produces another variation. To carry on this artifice in every part, Raphael judged it expedient to have the same number of figures in each groupe; but whereas in the principal one there are three heads between that of John and the column, and none between that of his and Peter's, so in this there appears but a part of one between the woman and the column, and the other three are placed in the space between the man and woman. The same artifice is also finely kept up in the distant colonnade; where, in the same space, two rows of the same columns appear in perspective, and by their contrast occasion the distance between the columns on the opposite side to appear larger than it really is. In short, this Cartoon is altogether the most consummate piece of art that probably ever was or ever will be produced.

CARTOON IV

THE DEATH OF ANANIAS

But Peter said, Ananias, why hath Satan filled thine heart to lie to the Holy Ghost, and to keep back part of the price of the land? Whilst it remained, was it not thine own? And after it was sold, was it not in thine own power? Why hast thou conceived this thing in thine heart? Thou hast not lied unto men, but unto God. And Ananias hearing these words fell down, and gave up the ghost. And great fear came on all that heard these things.—ACTS V. 3–5

OF ALL THE various ways ordained by the Almighty for putting a period to the present existence of human nature, there is none so affecting or alarming as the stroke of sudden death; whenever, therefore this happens, it appears more or less terrible to those who survive, according to the state of the soul at that moment when it is separated from the body. The death of Ananias was, therefore, a subject capable of exciting horror in an extraordinary degree, supposing it to have been only a common accident: but the circumstance of his death was much more terrifying, as it was a manifestation of the divine wrath upon him, "who had not lied unto men, but unto God." This alarming event happened at a time when the minds of the people were filled with the amazing things which they both saw and heard; when universal benevolence possessed the hearts of those who adhered to the doctrine taught by the apostles. Therefore such an event must have struck those who were witnesses to it with horror and reverence; with detestation of the act itself, and with reverential awe for the apostle, whose fore-knowledge of the fraud practised by Ananias, made him openly accuse him in the words above mentioned. Raphael has told this story in a manner worthy of his sublime genius; and the time chosen is so very evident that it need not be mentioned.

This Cartoon is composed of three distinct groupes, and Ananias is the principal figure; but it required no less than the profound skill of this great master to make him appear so; the figure being prostrate by necessity, must have appeared to some disadvantage, had the spectators been all standing, even though they had inclined as much as the two men who are stooping over him. Raphael, therefore, has most judiciously given all the figures in the forepart of the picture such attitudes, as at once perfectly correspond with the story, and make the figure of Ananias more conspicuous. Accordingly, the subordinate figures are all either kneeling or stooping; and these, at the same time, give an inexpressible dignity to the apostles, who are standing, and form a distinct groupe in the middle of the back part of the picture, in the centre of which Peter is placed, who is described as having just pronounced the accusation. The whole figure of Ananias is inimitably fine; but the expression in his character is amazing. There appears to be strongly marked in the features not only the stroke of death as a corporeal suffering, but the agonies of a wounded conscience; from which immediately proceeds the writhing contortions of the body and limbs the very extremities of which appear contracted and convulsed. The character of Peter is also finely imagined and designed: there is a holy severity in his countenance which is inexpressibly great; his attitude is majestic; and though his situation is something remote, it is impossible to avoid seeing that his is the second principal figure in the picture. The whole groupe of apostles are characters of great dignity; each seems collected within himself, and revolving upon this terrible catastrophe: and one of them, who is next to Peter, appears with reverential awe to address himself to the Almighty, and is a fine character. Horror, fear, and amazement, are blended in the character of the man who is opposed to Ananias; who by his situation and attitude appears also to be rendering up his goods to the apostles, and possibly was intended for Joses called Barnabas, who is mentioned in the latter part of the preceding chapter and this figure makes the finest contrast imaginable to that of the dying man. The woman next to him discovers her terror in a manner perfectly adapted to her sex, as well as the circumstances of the story. Her fear compels her to turn round, the natural preparative for flight; and this occasions her figure to contrast that of the man before described in a fine manner. The character of John, who is very properly employed in relieving the necessitous persons who compose a part of one of the subordinate groupes, is extremely graceful; compassion and benevolence are strongly expressed in his countenance, and his action discovers, that he not only relieves them with money, but likewise bestows with it his advice, and appears to exhort them to make a proper use of it. The apostle, who seems to beckon to some who are supposed to be out of the picture, to bear testimony of the punishment inflicted on Ananias, is a character of great dignity, and his attitude is finely varied from that of Peter's.

The draperies in this Cartoon are perfectly fine, and extremely well cast; particularly those of the apostles, which are remarkably graceful, and the folds finely disposed and contrasted. That of Ananias requires particular observation: he has less than any other figure in the picture, his arms, legs, and feet being entirely naked. This possibly to some may appear absurd, but it is a fine artifice; the violent agitation of the muscles is thereby made apparent; and the limbs of the figures near him being mostly covered, serve to shew his figure more distinctly, and of course help to discover its consequence. In short, the whole composition of this picture is perfectly great and striking, and is a remarkable instance of the genius of Raphael. In the Cartoon of the lame man healed, there is a luxury of fancy displayed in the ornaments with which it is enriched; in this its grandeur, dignity and effect, are totally derived from the invention and disposition of the characters. Ornaments there are none, and the bye-works are extremely plain and agreeable to the simplicity of the church of Christ in its infant state; the chief of them is the curtain, which is behind the apostles; it is indeed simple, but then it is finely folded and serves admirably to break the straight line, which is made by the heads of the apostles, which without this help, must have appeared somewhat disagreeably. The back ground is also artfully varied, and relieved by an opening on one side, and a flight of steps, with figures ascending them, on the other.

CARTOON V

ELYMAS THE SORCERER STRUCK WITH BLINDNESS

And now behold the hand of the Lord is upon thee; and thou shalt be blind, not seeing the light of the sun for a season. And immediately there fell on him a mist and a darkness, and he went about seeking some to lead him by the hand.—ACTS XIII. 11

THOUGH TERROR and astonishment are strongly expressed in this picture, yet it appears of a different kind, and produces a different effect from that in the Cartoon of the Death of Ananias. The punishment of Elymas was to him dreadful and grievous, and to the beholders terrifying and wonderful; but is apparently considered by them no otherwise than as it relates to this instance of the divine judgment inflicted on him. The death of Ananias inspired horror also, not without a mixture of pity for the sufferer, who, before the discovery of his crime, was probably esteemed as a good and devout man; on the contrary, the sorcerer was a person, of whom it may reasonably be judged the people stood in awe; and that he was rather feared on account of his power than beloved for his virtues. This will evidently appear, when the manner in which Raphael has told this story is considered. Every one of the spectators discovers terror and surprise; but none (except one of the lictors, who stands near the proconsul) discovers the least expression of pity. Elymas, though in the midst of numbers, appears to be alone: and he extends his arms in vain, "seeking some to lead him by the hand;" nor does the admirable figure, who stands between him and the proconsul, and who, with the utmost amazement, looks steadfastly in his face, seem inclinable to offer him the least assistance. Indeed, there are but few of the spectators who appear to give any attention at all to him; the majority of them being employed either in relating, or attending to the relation of the punishment inflicted upon him. Elymas who is the principal figure in this picture, according to the observation of Mr. Richardson, is blind from head to foot, and is altogether a most inimitable character. Perhaps Raphael hardly ever conceived one more expressive; and though this great master thought proper to assist the understanding by making the subordinate figures more fully explain the principal subject, yet this figure was alone sufficient to have done it. Dejected arrogance is amazingly described in his character, together with that shame and confusion, which must naturally have appeared in it when he felt the irresistible force and superiority of the divine power. His attitude is also extremely fine, and can only be thoroughly understood by viewing the picture itself, or a good copy or print after it. The apostle Paul is the next principal figure; he is placed opposite to the sorcerer, and is represented with one arm extended, as having just denounced sentence upon him, to the execution of which with a look of holy satisfaction, he seems to demand the proconsul's attention. He is likewise distinguished by a book, which he holds under the other arm. In his character, which appears in profile, the expression is awful and majestic; his whole figure is finely imagined and drawn, full of dignity and perfectly graceful. The next is the proconsul Sergius Paulus, who is more affected than any of the spectators: terror and astonishment are expressed in his countenance, and evidently discover that he feels the force, and is sensible of the equity of the divine judgment; but it appears in a manner perfectly becoming his character, and he sits amazed at the punishment of Elymas, and convinced of the truth of the doctrine preached by the holy apostles. The apostle Barnabas, who stands behind the sorcerer, is employed in explaining his fate to those who, by their situation, must necessarily be ignorant of it, as being placed behind him, which he is represented as doing with great zeal and energy. The man, who stands between Elymas and the proconsul, is prodigiously fine; he is, indeed, all amazement and attention; and in his character there is expressed a mixture of doubt, and an eagerness to discover whether the sorcerer's blindness is real or not. The man, whose head appears between that of Paul and the side of the picture, is also full of expression; he is apparently a believer, which is shewn by a fine mixture of fear and devotion in his countenance. There is likewise great expression in the lictors, who stand upon the steps; and also in the rest of the characters which compose this picture. The draperies in general are extremely fine, particularly that of Paul, which is noble, well-cast, and folded: that of the sorcerer is also finely imagined, and suitable to his character. The scenery or background of this Cartoon is magnificent, and well adapted; it will be sufficient to say that in order to break the stiffness of uniformity, Raphael has taken some liberties in the architecture, which produce an effect that makes ample amends for any seeming irregularity.

CARTOON VI

PAUL AND BARNABAS AT LYSTRA

And there sat a certain man at Lystra, impotent in his feet, being a cripple from his mother's womb, who never had walked. The same heard Paul speak, who steadfastly beholding him, and perceiving that he had faith to be healed, said with a loud voice, Stand upright on thy feet; and he leaped and walked. And when the people saw what Paul had done, they lifted up their voices, saying in the speech of Lycaonia, the gods are come down to us in the likeness of men. And they called Barnabas Jupiter, and Paul Mercurius, because he was chief speaker. Then the priest of Jupiter, which was before their city, brought oxen and garlands into the gates, and would have done sacrifice with the people. Which when the apostles Barnabas and Paul heard of, they rent their clothes, and ran in among the people, crying out.—ACTS XIV. 8–14

IN THIS CARTOON the simplicity and purity of the Christian religion is finely opposed to the pompous idolatry and superstition of the heathens: the divine behaviour and modesty of the two apostles is infinitely more striking and greater than all the tumult and parade of the sacrifice, which the priests, attended by the people, are about to make to them. The manner in which Raphael has described this ceremony, is perfectly fine, and agreeable to the custom of the Romans; and is entirely taken from the bass-relief of the Trajan column, the priests and boys employed in the intended sacrifice being almost exactly copied from thence, particularly the priest of Jupiter, who is in all respects, except in the drapery, the figure in the column being without any. In the characters of the priests and people there is a general expression of enthusiasm and superstitious fear, which is finely described. Paul is the principal figure in this picture: he is represented as standing upon a kind of step, from whence he is about to descend, in order to stop the mistaken religious fury of the people; and at the same time with the utmost grief and perturbation, which is admirably expressed, in his countenance, is rending his garment, and exposes part of his breast, which produces a fine effect in the imagination. The apostle Barnabas, who stands behind him, is a fine character; he is seen entirely in shadow; but his attitude and expression are incomparable; grief and pity are blended in his countenance, and he clasps his hands together with a fervour not to be described. Mr. Richardson, in speaking of this Cartoon, and the sacrifice represented in it, says, "the occasion of all that is finely told. The man who was healed of his lameness, is one of the forwardest to express his sense of the divine power, which appeared in those apostles; and to shew it to be him, not only a crutch is under his feet on the ground, but an old man takes up the lappet of his garment, and looks upon the limb, which he remembered to have been crippled, and expresses great devotion and admiration; which sentiments are also seen in the other, with a mixture of joy." Mr. Richardson might have added gratitude also, which is visibly expressed in the character of the cripple. And, indeed, if it be allowable to censure so great a master, the place in which this man is found is liable to some objection. Paul, in looking steadfastly upon him, perceived "he had faith to be healed;" and he is here represented among the crowd of idolaters, and appears to be one of the most zealous to assist at a ceremony so utterly disagreeable to his holy benefactors. To this it may be objected, that as he probably had not had time to be fully instructed in the Christian faith, this was the only way in which he could possibly testify his gratitude; but it is submitted whether he might not, with more propriety and equal advantage to the picture, have been introduced in the place of the man, who is on the same side of the picture with the apostles, employed in bringing a ram to the sacrifice; or at least in some other situation, in this particular more agreeable to his disposition to receive the religion of Christ. The whole figure of this man is finely designed, and vastly expressive; but the leg, which the old man is looking at, is remarkably elegant, and was undoubtedly painted from nature. The figure of the old man is also finely drawn and imagined, and his attitude, which is stooping, brings several subordinate figures into view, which could not otherwise have been seen. The architecture in the back ground of this Cartoon is magnificent; the forms of the buildings are finely varied; and the whole together exhibits a noble composition.

CARTOON VII

PAUL PREACHING AT ATHENS

Then Paul stood in the midst of Mars hill, and said, Ye men of Athens, I perceive that in all things ye are too superstitious: For as I passed by and beheld your devotions, I found an altar with this inscription, TO THE UNKNOWN GOD; *whom, therefore, ye ignorantly worship, him declare I unto you.*—ACTS XVII. 22, 23

IF INVENTION, expression, design, variety, and decorum, are allowed to constitute a fine historical composition, this Cartoon certainly deserves the character it has long maintained, of being one of the greatest performances of Raphael.

This fine picture is divided into three groupes; the first of which is composed of four figures, among whom the apostle is eminently distinguished, as indeed he is from every other in the picture; his situation being so extremely remarkable, that he is shewn to the greatest advantage that can possibly be conceived. The man who is about to ascend the steps, the woman behind him, and eight other figures who are represented standing, compose the second groupe; and the third is formed by six persons who are sitting. This last is placed between the first and second, nearly in the centre of the picture.

The character of Paul is universally allowed to be the most sublime performance that ever was produced by the pencil of Raphael; and Mr. Richardson, who passionately admired this figure, with a warmth peculiar to himself (which, perhaps, upon this, and some similar occasions carried him a little too far), says, "But no historian or orator, can possibly give me so great an idea of that eloquent and zealous apostle, as that figure of his does; all the fine things related, as said or wrote by him, cannot; for there I see a person, face, air, and action, which no words can sufficiently describe, but which assure me as much as those can, that that man must speak good sense, and to the purpose." Thus much is beyond contradiction, that nothing hitherto produced can give so great an idea of the person of Paul, or can better help to illustrate the divine zeal and elocution which that apostle so eminently possessed, than the awful, majestic, and expressive character, which the hand of Raphael has given them.

Raphael has employed every artifice, in order to make the apostle particularly conspicuous; all the figures in the picture are subservient to that purpose; the man and woman at the bottom of the steps are actually nearer to the eye than the apostle, but their situation causes the base line of the picture to cut off part of their height and as they are both stooping, they are effectually prevented from lessening the importance of the apostle. He has managed the figures that appear behind the apostle in the same manner, by placing two of them lower than Paul, and the third sitting upon the upper step; by which means they are sufficiently degraded. The figures in the second groupe, who are seen standing, are situated upon the ground, their heads mostly inclined, and are also at a considerable distance; and those who compose the middle groupe are at a still greater distance and are represented sitting. But the gigantic statue of Mars, which is introduced with great propriety is of infinite service to the picture; it is placed beyond the outermost figures of the second groupe; therefore the distance of this statue being considered, and the height and bulk of it compared with the figure of the apostle, it will be found to reduce the last to a moderate size, and also serves admirably, by its magnitude, to balance that side of the picture.

Among a great variety of fine characters in this picture, next to that of the apostles, is that of the man who is ascending the steps, in whose countenance awe and reverence are finely blended; nor need the most common observer be told, that this man and the woman behind him are intended to represent Dionysius and Damarius, who we are informed by the history were converted.

The expression of extreme attention in the three figures nearest to Dionysius in the second groupe, is most admirably described; nor is that of the man in the same groupe, who presses his lips with his finger, less to be admired. The three figures behind the apostle, who are apparently displeased with his discourse, are finely invented, particularly that of him who is sitting and rests his chin upon his hand; in his character envy and malignity are finely described.

Leonardo da Vinci, in his treatise upon Painting, has given it as a precept, that "In grave and serious compositions, when assemblies are held, and matters of importance debated, let but few young men be present; it being contrary to custom to intrust affairs of this nature in the hands of youth, who are not less able to give counsel, than they are willing to receive it; and who, therefore, have two reasons for absenting themselves from these kinds of meetings." This precept is no where better illustrated than in this Cartoon, where there is a wonderful expression of attention, decorum, and gravity, in the old men; and, on the contrary, the few young persons who are introduced in the picture appear forward, impatient, and impetuous, and contempt and dislike are strongly expressed in each of their characters; for which reason part of these turbulent persons are judiciously thrown into the most distant groupe, and others are placed behind the older men.

In the distance between the buildings, in the center of the picture, are seen two figures, who appear to be talking together, and seem to be of no consequence to the composition; but their use is great: they not only serve to break the straight line made by the heads of those who are sitting, as also the parallel lines made by the columns of the temple and the adjacent piazza, but connect the principal and two subordinate groupes together; and without them the picture must have suffered considerably.

The attitudes of the figures are extremely fine and expressive; the draperies noble and well cast, particularly that of the apostle, which is admirably designed. The architecture is elegant, not rich, but suitable to the taste of the Athenians, and properly adapted to the picture; as is the distant view of the country, it being customary for them to place the statue of Mars, as the guardian of the city, at the entrance into it.

Upon the whole, it may not be improper to conclude, with comparing the ideas of two such great painters as Raphael and Leonardo da Vinci in similar subjects, by the following extract from the writings of the latter, who, in describing the manner in which a public oration should be represented, says, "To represent a person haranguing a multitude, consider, in the first place, the subject-matter on which he is to entertain them, in order to give him an action suitable to the occasion; for instance, if the business be to persuade, let it appear in his gestures; if it be to argue and deduce reasons, let him hold one of the fingers of his left hand between two of those of the right, keeping the other two shut; let his face be turned to the assembly, and his mouth half open, so that he may appear to speak; if he be sitting, let him seem as about to rise, advancing his head a little forwards; if he be represented standing let him incline a little with his head and breast towards the people; and let the assembly be seen listening with silence and attention; let all their eyes be fastened on the speaker, and let their actions discover somewhat of admiration; let some old man be seen wondering at what he hears, with his mouth shut, his lips drawn close, wrinkles about the corners of his mouth, the bottom of his cheeks, and in the forehead, occasioned by the eyebrows, which must be raised near the setting on of the nose; let others be represented sitting, with their fingers clasped within each other, bearing up their left knee, another old man may be seen with his knees thrown across each other, his elbow leaning on his knee, and with his hand supporting his chin, which may be covered with a venerable beard."

The similarity of the ideas of these two great men will be better discovered by comparing the Cartoon with the foregoing quotation, where, though several things are differently expressed, yet upon the whole, the thought is so nearly alike, that it may be almost implied, that either Leonardo's idea had been put in execution by Raphael, or, could there have been a probability of it, that the latter had dictated to the former when he was composing his book.

APOSTLES IN ENGLAND

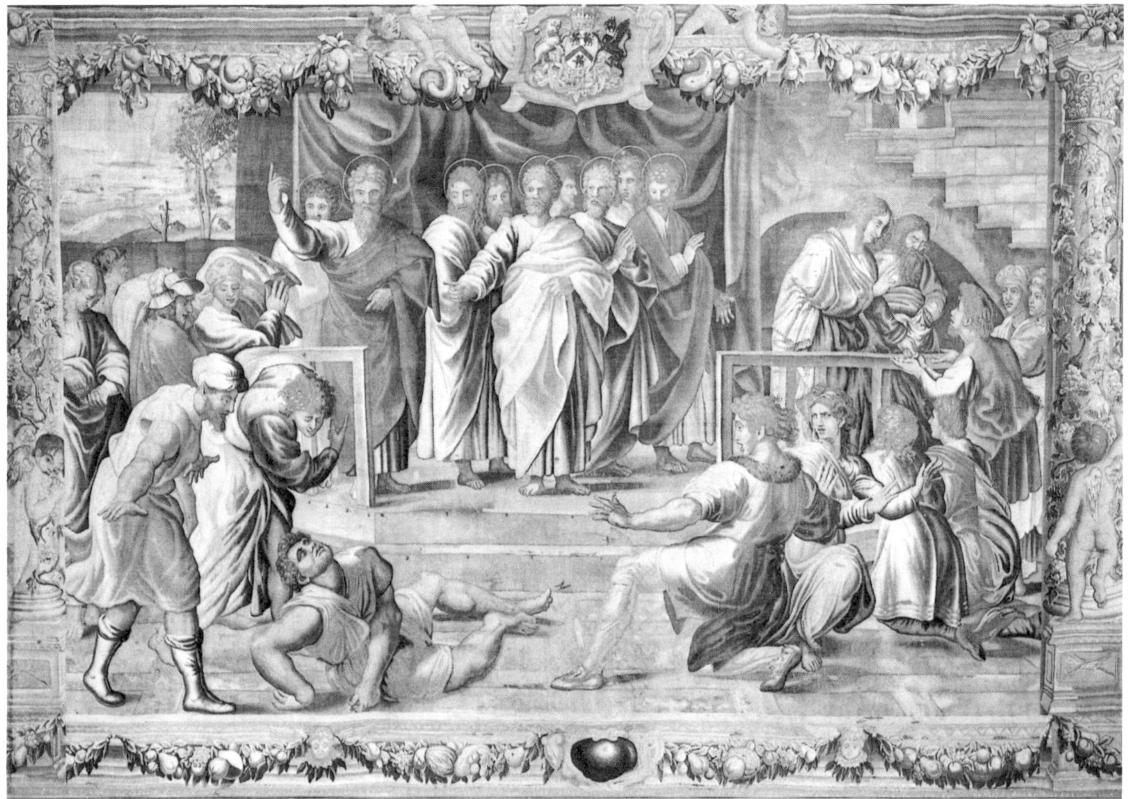

FIG. 10 After Raphael, *The Death of Ananias*, ca.1685, Mortlake tapestry (*cat. 24*)

I. INTRODUCTION

As THE CURTAIN opened on the eighteenth century in England, Raphael began to occupy the same position in the visual arts that Sir Isaac Newton held in empirical science. Raphael's seven Tapestry Cartoons[1] depicting the Acts of the Apostles had just been installed in a new gallery at Hampton Court. From the moment they first hung as autonomous works, the Cartoons began to play an important role in furthering the progress of the arts in England. Raising the level of artistic taste and the performance of English artists were compelling issues of national pride during those early decades of the century. And in these normative models of Renaissance art, the English found those very qualities

1. The word "cartoon" traditionally means a preparatory design made to scale for a work that will be rendered in another medium such as in fresco, oil, or tapestry. In 1843, however, under the title "cartoons," *Punch* parodied Raphael's historical productions on the occasion of the competition for designs for frescoes in the new Houses of Parliament, and ever since the word has possessed the meaning we commonly associate with it today.

with which their national character had an affinity. It seems a curious contradiction, that given their Roman Catholic origin, Raphael's Cartoons helped to shape an aesthetic style that was solidly rooted in Anglican beliefs. Of course, English artists were keenly aware that the French had already made Raphael the basis of their academic system, and in the course of the century the English would lose no opportunity to triumph over *le Rafael gaulois.*

Raphael's Cartoons had originally been commissioned by Pope Leo X to be used as designs for a set of tapestries to hang in the Sistine Chapel.[2] Around 1515 they were sent to be woven by Pieter van Aelst in Brussels and, as was the practice, were cut into strips for use under the looms. In 1623 Charles, Prince of Wales (who became Charles I in 1625), purchased seven of the ten original Cartoons, which by that time had made their way to Genoa. In England they were put to the same use as in Brussels, and new sets of tapestries were woven at the Mortlake manufactory.

Among the more than one dozen sets of Raphael's tapestries made at Mortlake that can now be traced is that at the Cathedral of Saint John the Divine in New York (fig. 10) which formerly was at Burley-on-the-Hill, Leicestershire.[3] These post-Restoration weavings, made circa 1685, that is, before the Mortlake works closed in 1703, are in reverse of the Cartoons since weavers followed Raphael's designs through the horizontal warp on what would be the back of the tapestries.[4]

In 1699 the status of the Cartoons significantly changed when William III had the strips pieced back together, restored, and hung as autonomous works at Hampton Court. From that time, the prestige of the Cartoons began to surpass that of the tapestries. For English painters, the Cartoons were to become the canonical models of the classical style, while Raphael himself became the object of tributes that outstripped any reverence paid to a monarch or divine. The Cartoons were the only monumental works by Raphael to be seen outside of Rome in the first half of the eighteenth century. And ever since those seven extraordinary designs were first formally displayed in a gallery designed specifically for them by Sir Christopher Wren, they spawned generations of engraved and painted progeny.

Among their offspring are the seven half-size copies painted by Sir James Thornhill which

2. Raphael's Acts of the Apostles are depictions of episodes in the lives of Saint Peter and Saint Paul. Of the original ten designs, three no longer survive (*Stoning of Stephen*; *Conversion of Paul*; *Paul in Prison*) and are known only from the tapestries made from them. The story of the Cartoons and the tapestries has frequently been told, most comprehensively by J. Shearman, in *Raphael's Cartoons and the Tapestries for the Sistine Chapel*, London, 1972.

3. The set was sold at auction in London, 26 March 1953 (lot 86) and given to the cathedral the following year. Other cathedrals owning sets of the tapestries are at Beauvais, Bourges, and Loretto.

The borders bear the arms of the earldom of Winchelsea and Nottingham in the center of the top band, and most likely were designed by Francis Cleyn. According to the personal instructions of Lord Nottingham, and with the practical assistance of the tapestry maker Stephen Demay, the individual panels were considerably enlarged in 1700, and an eighth panel was added depicting *The Death of Sapphira* that has no counterpart in the Raphael Cartoons (Marillier, MS. Notes, and P. Finch, *History of Burley-on-the-Hill*, London, 1901, 1:92–96). This set comprises nine panels since *Christ's Charge to Peter* was woven in two separate sections.

4. The relation of a cartoon to a finished tapestry is substantially different from the relation of a finished drawing to an oil or fresco painting for which it serves as the model. Although both cases involve a translation from one medium to another, tapestry requires that the image be materially restructured in thread. The technical execution by specially trained craftsmen involves a major interpretative transformation. The relation between the cartoon and the tapestry, therefore, is more akin to that between a drawing and a sculpture, than between a drawing and a painting.

are the centerpiece of the current exhibition (figs. 1–7). In making these copies Thornhill intended to preserve for posterity what he believed had been lost from the originals through both the accidents of time and the hands of restorers.[5] During three unremunerated years in the Cartoon Gallery at Hampton Court (1729–31), he made several sets of copies after the Acts of the Apostles in various sizes. Thornhill's dedication to the project was born of an ongoing preoccupation with improving the training of British artists and of a more particular desire to make Raphael accessible to students. Produced some forty years prior to the founding of England's Royal Academy in 1768, Thornhill's paintings offer a unique opportunity to reconsider copying as not just a reproductive process but a didactic tool.

Before Thornhill took on the project of copying the Cartoons in 1729, he had been a successful decorative painter who worked in the grand manner and on a grand scale. His major commissions were linked to the architecture of Sir Christopher Wren and included the decoration of the Banqueting Hall of the Royal Naval College at Greenwich and the cupola of Saint Paul's Cathedral in London (figs. 71–73).[6] In light of the very slow revival of the arts in England after a long and disruptive period of civil war, Thornhill's artistic accomplishment seems remarkable. In the absence of an established tradition of artistic training, and with a dearth of first-rate pictures readily at hand to study and learn from, it took unusual energy and ambition to compete successfully with the allegories that rolled off the brushes of his Italian and French competitors in England—Sebastiano Ricci, Giovanni Pellegrini, Antonio Verrio, and Louis Laguerre.

Thornhill's oil copies of Raphael's Cartoons were given to the Department of Art History and Archaeology at Columbia in 1959 by Mrs. Francis Lenygon, thanks to Rudolph Wittkower, the noted scholar of baroque art who was then chairman, who fully appreciated their immense historical and artistic significance in eighteenth-century England. Until now, when they are being shown publicly for the first time, they have hung discreetly in several seminar and lecture rooms in Schermerhorn Hall. The general response to Thornhill's paintings has been neither approval nor rebuke but instead—and more damning—overwhelming indifference. This exhibition thus aims to spur a reexamination of these copies by presenting them within the context of the cultural and historical circumstances that generated not only these but so many other replications. Insofar as copies have always occupied something of a twilight zone in the realm of artistic creativity, my concern here is primarily with the polemical use of copies and the artistic ambitions underlying their production. It is these that tell the story of the second coming of Raphael's Apostles in England—and of their entry into aesthetic, political, and religious discourse.

5. Shearman, *Raphael's Cartoons*, 147, suggests that much of the repainting may have been done in the 1620s after the Cartoons first arrived in England.

6. The cupola was entirely repainted by E. T. Parris in 1853–56.

II. REGARDING COPIES

WHILE THE FORMAL DISPLAY at Hampton Court brought the Cartoons to the public's attention, it did not bring public access; it was primarily through engraved and painted reproductions that Raphael's ideas became widely known. Although engraved copies[7] after famous works were seen as small-scale *translations* into another medium, painted copies of the sort that Thornhill made—sometimes paradoxically termed "original copies"—were accepted as *substitutes* for the works they replicated. Such copies were concerned with "imitation" in the most literal sense of the term.[8] Insofar as they were "taken from the life," they were regarded as "portraits" of the originals and thus were "authentic" in themselves as well as testaments to the authenticity of the model.

The institutionalization during the latter decades of the seventeenth century of the practice of making painted copies after works by acknowledged masters was made possible by current painting theory. The idea that the pictorial conception of a painting was not only more important than but in fact independent of its mechanical execution meant that copies had much to recommend them. Painting theory sanctioned copying as an instructional aid, and the French Academy in Rome set the precedent for its extensive practice. Copying old-master paintings on a large scale became an integral part of the curriculum at the academy, where it served the dual function of providing Paris with duplicates of Rome's artistic treasures and, in the process, ostensibly training the young French pensioners who had won the Prix de Rome.

The first ambitious copying project undertaken at the French Academy was initiated in 1664 by Charles Errard when he was appointed director and involved producing full-size copies of Raphael's larger works, including the tapestries, in the Vatican. It is uncertain if the instructional use of the copies was assigned a higher priority than their commercial application in the manufacture of tapestries in France. Nonetheless, from a practical perspective—given the accepted premise that one first learns by imitating the masters—the copies served the training of students in Paris who did not have access to originals. The advantages of this enterprise were approvingly noted by the duc de Chaulnes in a letter to Colbert, minister to Louis XIV, after he had seen the Acts of the Apostles that academy students had copied from the tapestries in the Vatican:

> A few days ago I saw the copies that the painters of the Royal Academy have made of the tapestries after Raphael's designs; the work is one which has been carried out to perfection and which offers several advantages; the first, that the King may have more beautiful tapestries than those here; the second, that the paintings will be a beautiful ornament wherever they are hung; and the third, that they will serve as a school for painters where they will profit considerably.[9]

7. In its Latin etymology the word "copy" was associated with the notion of copiousness, and the advent of the printing press made not only words abundant but images as well. The print medium was a truly democratizing force, for it opened the previously privileged domain of visual ideas to a receptive and ever-widening audience. See M. de Grazia, *Shakespeare Verbatim: The Reproduction of Authenticity and the 1790 Apparatus*, Oxford, 1991, 89–92.

8. For a succinct discussion of copying tied to the theory of imitation, and of the practice of copying by Renaissance artists, which became the basis of all subsequent art education, see E. Haverkamp-Begemann, *Creative Copies*, exh. cat., The Drawing Center, New York, 1988, 13–21.

9. "Je vis, il y a quelques jours, les copies que les Peintres de l'Académie du Roy ont fait des tapisseries sur les desseins de Raphael; c'est un travail qui a ésté exécuté en perfection et

In addition to these works, which were sent to Paris toward the end of 1670,[10] eight of Raphael's Vatican frescoes had also been copied and woven in tapestry in France by 1691.[11] Since there were no paintings by Raphael in France at that time comparable to the frescoes in the Vatican Stanze,[12] they held a central place in the studies of the pensioners in Rome. Copying his large-scale works in the Vatican continued under Errard's successors, at least until 1705, when the Vatican closed its doors to students for twenty years. During this period,[13] the French were reduced to copying from the copies made by the pensioners who had been resident in Rome in earlier, more hospitable days.

It was during this rather dreary epoch of the French Academy in Rome that England began to appreciate the special advantage not only in having major works by Raphael on home soil but in having works of a caliber that could even rival those in the Vatican. Following the injunction of Anthony Ashley Cooper, third earl of Shaftesbury, to raise the arts in England by honing the nation's taste on judicious models,[14] the artist Jonathan Richardson was the most effective in directing painters and connoisseurs to the excellence of Raphael's Cartoons. It was in the wake of this instructional concern that Thornhill undertook to make his painted copies. For, although England was more fortunate than France in having important, large-scale originals at hand, the Cartoons were still not available to students.

While, thanks to the French example, copying was an established tenet of academic instruction, copying from *painted* copies was a practical necessity. Using prints was far more limiting, and the artistic validity of reproductive engravings was seriously questioned during the eighteenth century.[15] Their most obvious shortcoming was lack of color, although James Christopher Le Blon's experiments with color reproduction in the 1720s attempted to address this complaint.[16] Further objections involved the loss of painterly qualities and the lib-

dont l'on tirera plusieurs avantages: le premier que le Roy pourra avoir de plus belles tapisseries que celles qui sont icy; le deuxième, que les tableaux seront un bel ornemont partout où l'on voudra les mettre, et le troisième, que ce sera une ecolle pour les Peintres où ils pourront beaucoup proffiter" (11 February 1670), Montaignion, 1887, cited in J. P. Cuzin et al., *Raphael et l'art français*, exh. cat., Grand Palais, Paris, 1984, 244.

10. These copies were not used by the Gobelins manufactory in the seventeenth century but were sent to be woven at Beauvais around 1692 (Cuzin, *Raphael et l'art français*, 244).

11. Rosenberg 1995, 44, 46.

12. Three paintings by Raphael *(Saint Michael; Holy Family; Small Holy Family)* were the subjects of official academy lectures *(Conférences)* which were initiated in 1667 "to give an explanation of the best pictures from the King's collection" (J. Montagu, *The Expression of the Passions*, New Haven, 1994, 70 and n. 20). Students in Paris, however, could know most of Raphael's masterpieces only through copies.

13. This was under Charles Poerson's directorship of the French Academy in Rome (1704–25), when, for lack of funds and students, it was at its lowest ebb (Rosenberg 1995, 71). Poerson complained to Jules Hardouin-Mansart, "A l'esgard de la Peinture, les lieux où sont les belles chose qui ont acquis tant de réputation a cette ville son quazi touttes ruinée et de plus fermée aux étudiantes" (B. Hercenberg, *Nicolas Vleughels: Peintre et directeur de l'Academie de France à Rome, 1668–1737*, Paris, 1975, 17).

14. A. A. Cooper, third earl of Shaftesbury, *Characteristics of Men, Manners, Opinions, Times*, London, 1732, 1:338.

15. By Richardson, Bernard Picart, Francesco Algarotti, and others (C. Lloyd and T. Ledger, *Art and Its Images*, exh. cat., Bodleian Library, Oxford, 1975, 16). On the other hand, in the introduction to the *Cabinet de Crozat*, Paris, 1729, it was claimed that engraved reproductions were superior to painted copies because the latter were usually mediocre (S. Lambert, *The Image Multiplied*, London, 1987, 37).

16. Le Blon developed one of the earliest methods of color printing that used the three-color principle, derived from Newton's theory of light. His company in London was called the Picture Office, and his intention was to make color reproductions of the old masters that would have a presence comparable to that of the original. By 1722 Le Blon was accused of cheating his shareholders and was removed from his post as director (Lambert, *Image Multiplied*, 87).

erties often taken with composition.[17] Sanction for Thornhill's copying efforts could also be found in Richardson's contention that the best masters made the best copyists.[18] But later in the century—and at a point when there were still very few works to be used as instructional models at the recently founded Royal Academy—Sir Joshua Reynolds worried about copying as "a delusive kind of industry" that readily led to the dangerous habit of imitating without selecting.[19] In a direct reversal of the ideas promoted early in the century, Reynolds argued that the advantage of copying was not in the conceptual realm but rather in the mechanical practice of painting.[20]

III. EIGHTEENTH-CENTURY COPIES OF RAPHAEL'S TAPESTRY CARTOONS

THE FIRST ENGRAVINGS: SIMON GRIBELIN

THE ENGRAVER George Vertue (1684–1756), whose notebooks are a primary source for the history of the arts in England, described copper-plate engraving at the beginning of the eighteenth century as being at an unusually low ebb.[21] There seemed to be no one in line to replace those skillful masters of the previous generation like Gerard Edelinck in France (d. 1707) or Robert White in London (d. 1703). Vertue attributed this sorry state to a lack of adequate training in drawing, but he noted that of even greater consequence was the lack of any artistic exchange with France. This had became impossible around 1690, when war with France had virtually sealed off England's borders. Neither French engravers nor their prints crossed the Channel to England until the latter part of Queen Anne's reign (1702–14).[22]

The state of the art of engraving looked far more promising by the end of the first decade of the century, with the major commercial success of the first complete set of prints ever to have been made after Raphael's Tapestry Cartoons.[23] They were engraved in 1707 by the Huguenot Simon Gribelin (1661–1733), who by that time had been living in England for

17. Typically, this was a result of the collaborative effort required for the preparation of the plate which usually involved two or three people, thereby increasing the chance of misrepresentation in the course of the various intermediary stages of the reversal and transcription of the image (Lloyd and Ledger, *Art and Its Images*, 8).

18. Richardson 1773, 235.

19. Reynolds, 29.

20. Ibid., 30.

21. Vertue III, 7; Vertue VI, 184–86. For a full account of Vertue as a chronicler of the arts, see I. Bignamini, "George Vertue, Art Historian, and Art Institutions in London 1689–1768," *Walpole Society*, LIV, 1991, 2–19. Upon Vertue's death, Horace Walpole acquired his notebooks and brought order and method to Vertue's invaluable but seemingly random jottings in the *Anecdotes on Painting in England.* Walpole was dismayed by the confusion of Vertue's notes: "There are forty manuscript volumes of Vertue's collections, all entered without method and without any direction for finding anything" (letter of 10 May 1766, J. Hutchins, *The History and Antiquities of the County of Dorset*, London, 1796–1815, 2:461–63).

22. Consequently, painters such as Verrio and Laguerre who decorated England's palaces and country houses in the grand baroque style could find no one to engrave their designs.

23. Vertue III, 7.

almost thirty years.[24] This was indeed a period of great artistic opportunity in England, and even Vertue expressed surprise at the rapid rise of his own reputation as an engraver.

Gribelin's engravings (figs. 11, 15) were advertised in 1709 in the *Tatler* as "seven very large sheet prints . . . Each print 26" long and 23" deep."[25] These measurements are deceptive, however, since they give the size of the full sheet of printing paper, and the plates themselves were in fact only 7 1/4 by 8 1/2 inches. Ultimately, their very small scale was judged too mean to do justice either to Raphael's compositional invention or to his compelling repertoire of expressions. Falling far short of a dignified tribute to that Renaissance master, Gribelin's prints served primarily as pocket reminders of Raphael's prowess.

Gribelin's talent was better suited to the goldsmith's art of ornamental engraving on silver and on other small items such as watchcases and snuff boxes. He even published several pattern books of intricate designs adaptable as decorative plates for publishers.[26] But the recognition he had received in 1693 from engraving Charles Le Brun's historically important painting *The Tent of Darius* (fig. 45) encouraged his further efforts in reproductive engraving.[27]

In 1720 Gribelin's set of Raphael's Cartoons was reissued with an eighth page carrying a portrait and a dedication to "Her late Majesty, Queen Anne."[28] This elaborate frontispiece (fig. 8), ornamented at the top with Raphael's portrait borne aloft on a swag of drapery by cupids,[29] shows a full and faithful view of the Cartoons as they were installed in the Gallery at Hampton Court. When the individual plates of the Cartoons were engraved, however, they were not reversed, and thus the set is shown in the same orientation as the woven tapestries rather than of the original Cartoons. Additionally, Gribelin took liberties with their

24. Gribelin had come to England in 1680, became a citizen the following year, and was admitted into the Clockmaker Company in 1686. His original drawings, executed in pencil, inked over and with some red chalk, are in the collection at Windsor Castle (cat. no. 163: 17314–17321). A. P. Oppé (*English Drawings at Windsor*, London, 1950, 53–54, no. 278) fails to mention the engravings of 1707 and refers only to the undated set of engravings after these drawings which were published for John Bowles in 1720. J. D. Passavant, also only mentions the set published in 1720 (*Raphael d'Urbin et son père*, Paris, 1860, 2:208).

25. No. 69, 17 September 1709. Gribelin was not identified as the engraver in the advertisement, which simply stated the plates were "engraved by a very good hand." They were sold by Henry Overton, Print and Map Seller at the White Horse without Newgate.

26. His grandfather had been watchmaker to Louis XIII, and his father, Jacob Gribelin, had been an engraver in Blois. He published pattern books in 1682 and 1697 and *A New Book of Ornaments; Useful to All Artists* in 1704.

27. Walpole 1763, 107–8, incorrectly dates Gribelin's engraving of *The Tent of Darius* to 1707. It was published in 1693 and accompanied André Félibien's *Tent of Darius Explain'd or the Queen of Persia at the Feet of Alexander*, trans. Col. Parsons, London, 1703. Vertue, however, was particularly indignant about the inscription, which claimed that it was "d'après le Tableau qu'en fait par Mr. Le Brun," when it was publicly known that Gribelin's version was derived from the print that Edelinck had engraved in Paris from the original (Vertue III, 106).

28. The first issue of the prints carries a simple letterpress title page with a dedication to Queen Anne. The drawing at Windsor for the later title page carries two earlier drafts of penciled inscriptions, both of which are canceled. A print of the title page at the Victoria and Albert Museum is inscribed with incomplete dates in English and in Latin, suggesting a date prior to 1709: the date engraved in the English inscription, "170," omits the final digit, and in the Latin inscription reads "Ann: MDCCV," which can also be regarded as incomplete, since the addition of I, II, or III could extend the date up to 1708 without requiring a burnished correction. Elizabeth Miller (letter 3 April 1996) has suggested that this lettering may have been altered after some of the impressions taken around 1720 were printed in order to produce a rare state.

29. A similar swag of drapery is borne aloft by virtually the same team of cupids at the top of *The Adoration* that Thornhill painted on the east wall of the chapel at Wimpole Hall (1724).

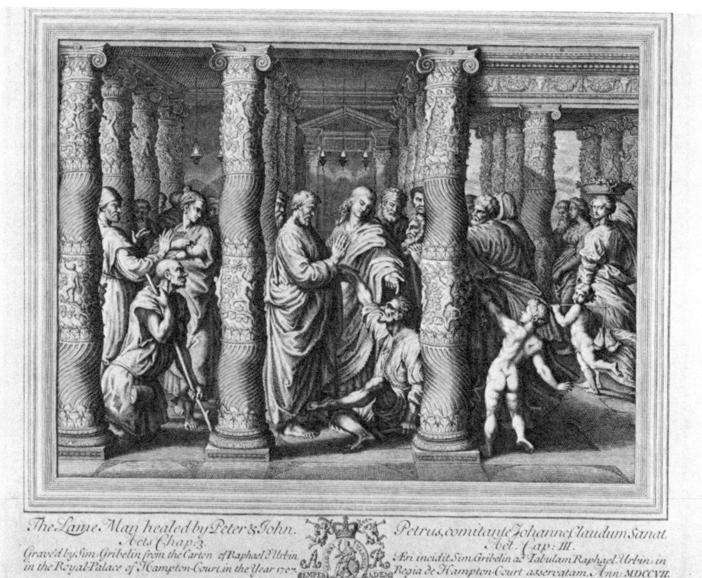

FIG. 11 Simon Gribelin (after Raphael), *The Lame Man Healed* (1707), 1720 (*cat. 9c*)

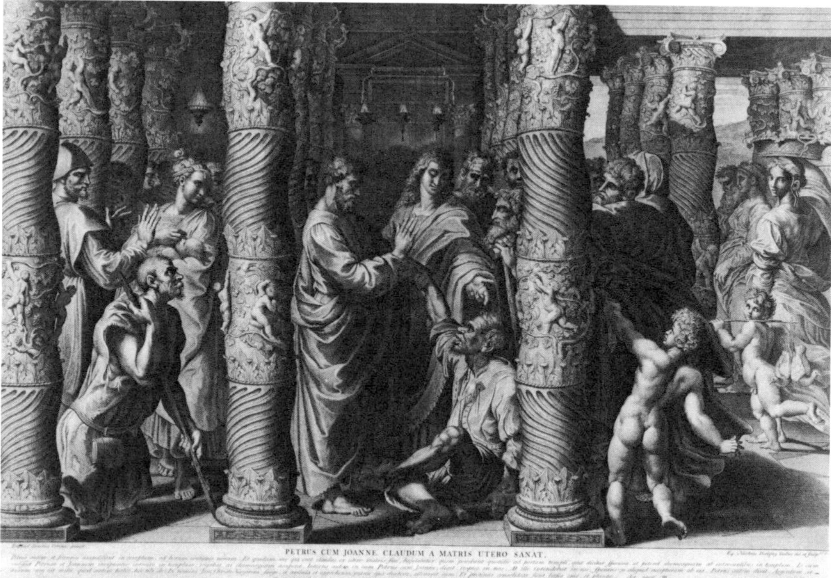

FIG. 12 Nicolas Dorigny (after Raphael), *The Lame Man Healed,* 1719 (*cat. 4c*)

true proportions, which he altered in order to produce a uniform set of prints. This tidy regularization suggests that his notions about engraving were very much conditioned by book production.[30]

Most virtuosi found Gribelin's Raphael prints wanting despite their commercial success. One exception was Lord Shaftesbury, who after viewing a sample print enlisted Gribelin to provide engravings for the second edition of his *Characteristics of Men, Manners, Opinions, Times.*[31] Far more critical was Jonathan Richardson's assessment of Gribelin as "a careful la-

30. In *A New Book of Ornaments* (see n. 26) Gribelin explained that "these XVI plates are now made up into one book of XII leaves and the 8 small ones are thus printed to make the whole more regular."

31. Shaftesbury wrote from Naples to Thomas Micklewayte (2 February 1712), asking that he be sent at least a single print from the set of Cartoons to see "what the Learn'd here think of M. Gribelin's hand for Engravery in real Figures and History" (S. O'Connell, "Lord Shaftesbury in Naples, 1711–1713," *Walpole Society,* LIV, 1991, 162).

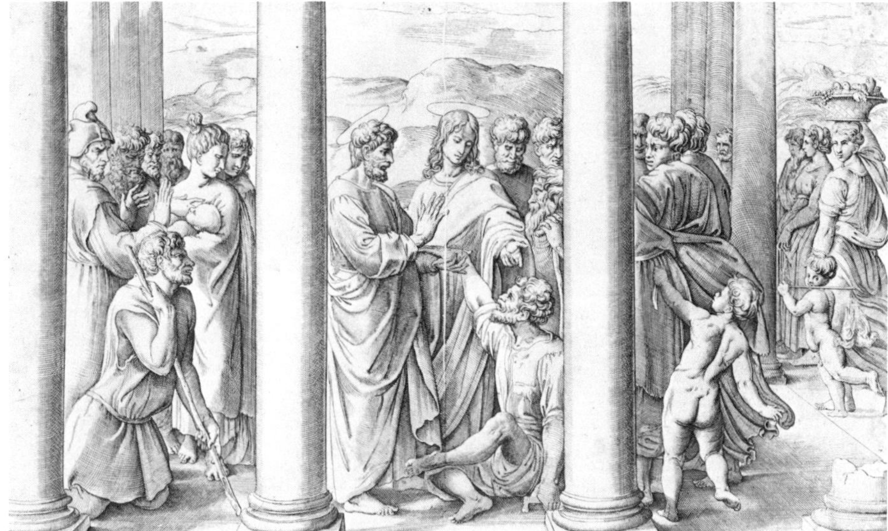

FIG. 13 Giovanni Battista Franco (after Raphael), *The Lame Man Healed*, mid century (*cat. 6*)

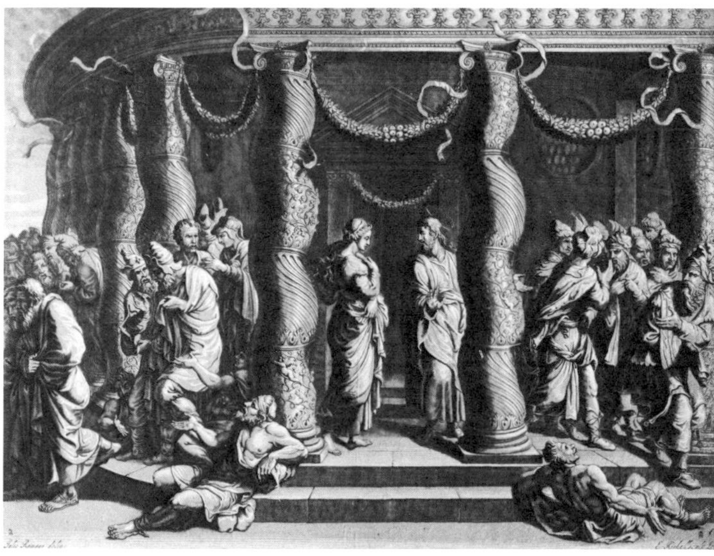

FIG. 14 Elisha Kirkall (after Giulio Romano, after Raphael), *Disputation in the Temple*, 1722 (*cat. 15*)

borious engraver, of no extensive genius, but painfully exact."[32] Walpole, too, found Gribelin lacking both in his manner and in his capacity and mustered only a modicum of praise for his fastidiousness. At best, Walpole considered the engravings "neat memorandums," diminutive transcriptions that could scarcely do justice to Raphael's compositions. But his main complaint—and here he also cited prints after pictures by old masters in the royal collection[33] and after the painted ceiling of the Banqueting House by Rubens—was that none of Gribelin's plates ever gave any idea of the style of the artists he copied.[34]

32. Richardson 1792, 263.

33. These included paintings by Tintoretto, Schiavone, Jacobo Palma, Giulio Romano, and Veronese. A presentation volume at Windsor Castle, dedicated to George, Prince of Wales, dated March 1715, comprises more than thirty-five engravings by Gribelin.

34. Walpole 1763, 107–8. On this score, Gribelin's engravings should be compared with the two Cartoons that Gérard Audran engraved about five years earlier (see pp. 32–33).

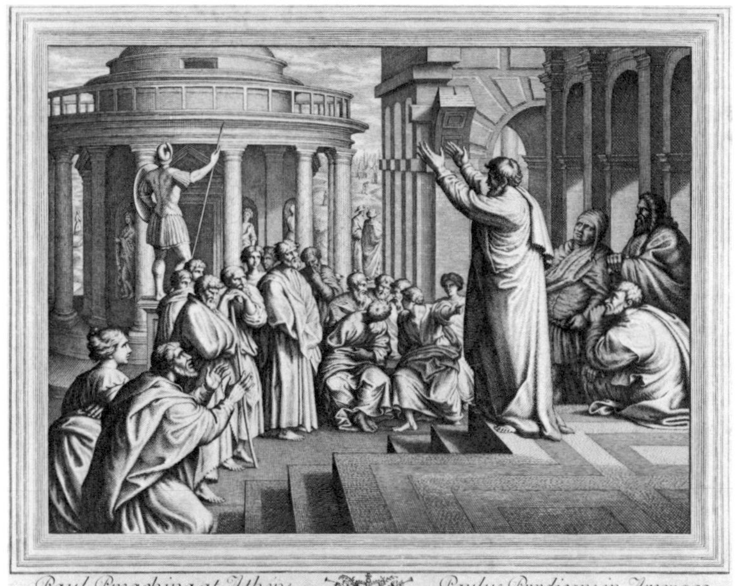

FIG. 15 Simon Gribelin (after Raphael), *Paul Preaching at Athens* (1707), 1720 (*cat. 9g*)

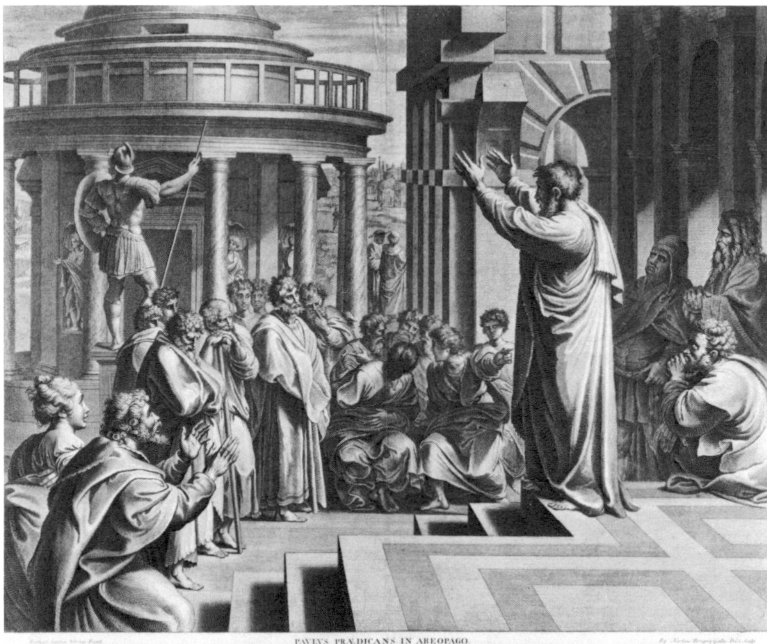

FIG. 16 Nicolas Dorigny (after Raphael), *Paul Preaching at Athens*, 1719 (*cat. 4g*)

Nevertheless, the very considerable sales of Gribelin's prints, despite the shortcoming of their quarto format, opened the door for the more formidable folio edition that followed.[35]

35. When other sets of engravings came on the market, the price of Gribelin's set progressively dropped. In 1754 the print publisher Henry Overton listed them in his catalogue under "Cheap Sets of Prints" (E. Miller, "From Marcantonio Raimondi to the Postcard: Prints of the Raphael Cartoons," exh. checklist, Victoria and Albert Museum, London, 1995).

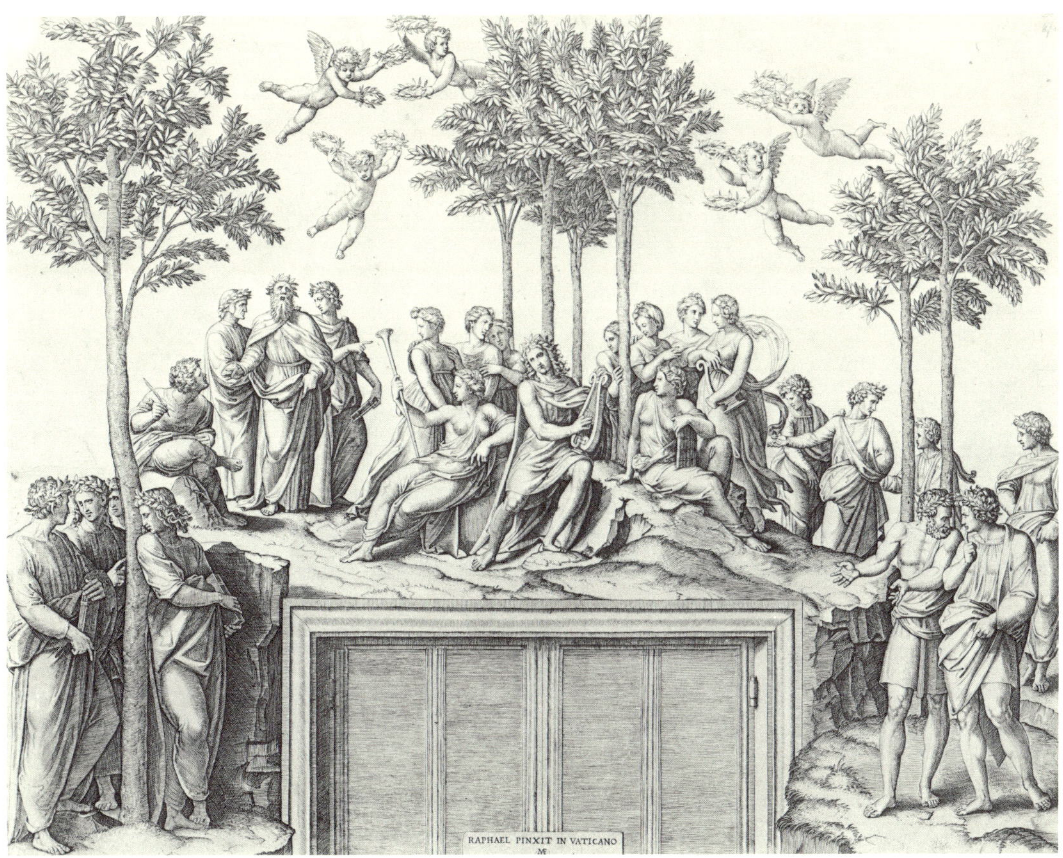

FIG. 17 Marcantonio Raimondi (after Raphael), *Parnassus*, ca.1517–20 (*cat. 22*)

"PINACOTHECA HAMPTONIANA": NICOLAS DORIGNY'S FOLIO EDITION

According to Vertue, the true rise in the art of engraving in England could be charted from the arrival of Nicolas Dorigny (1658–1746) in 1711.[36] Dorigny's reputation as the first engraver in Europe was secured by his engravings after Raphael's Cupid and Psyche cycle in the Farnesina, which were issued in an impressive folio edition in 1693,[37] and by a much lauded print of Raphael's *Transfiguration* in 1705.[38]

36. Vertue IV, 187. Although Dorigny's grandfather (on his mother's side) was Simon Vouet, his early professional training was in law. At about age thirty, when a hearing defect precluded pursuing that career, Dorigny went to Italy to study painting, joining his elder brother who had been a pupil of Le Brun. Writing with the vested interest of a fellow engraver, Vertue relates many details about the difficult course of Dorigny's progress in etching and engraving, not least of all the competition he suffered from an engraver named Van Oudenarde, who enjoyed the protection and encouragement of the influential Maratta (Vertue I, 51).

The very year of his arrival in England Dorigny was listed as one of the directors of the newly formed academy in Great Queen Street.

37. *Psyches et Amoris Nuptiae ac Fabula a Raphaele Sanctio Urbinate Romae in Farnesianis Hortis . . .*

38. Vertue IV, 186–87. Addison considered Dorigny's engraving after *The Transfiguration* "the noblest print in the world." With somewhat more restraint, Richardson simply judged it his very best performance (Richardson 1792, 263).

As the story is told, the carrot used to lure Dorigny to England to engrave the Tapestry Cartoons was royal patronage, apparently offered by some admiring (but unnamed) gentlemen during a visit to Rome.[39] It is likely that one of those gentleman was John Talman, the well-connected son of the leading Whig architect during William III's reign, who upon arriving in Italy in 1709 became intensely involved in the artistic scene and in overseeing ambitious engraving projects.[40]

When Dorigny arrived in London in June of 1711 it was presumed that the Crown would bear the expense of engraving the plates, since the sets of prints were to be given as gifts to foreign princes and ministers. But Dorigny's demand of some £4,000–5,000 was regarded as an untenable public expense, notwithstanding the support of Robert Harley, lord treasurer to Queen Anne. The Queen did provide the engraver with an apartment at Hampton Court and the necessary perquisites–firewood and a bottle of wine daily. Forced to raise money himself to underwrite the project, Dorigny was unable to begin work until the spring of the following year.[41]

Dorigny advertised a "Proposal for Graving and Printing the Gallery of Raphael at Hampton Court" in the *Daily Courant* on 25 October 1711, offering subscriptions for eight plates nineteen inches high and from twenty-five to thirty inches long. He claimed that by setting the price at a modest four guineas a set he aimed at reputation rather than profit, noting that this was well below the twenty guineas for which his five prints of Alexander's battles after paintings by Le Brun frequently sold.

His appeal for funds was promoted by Richard Steele in the *Spectator* which the Rev. Gunn would later call "one of the most dignified advertisements ever penned."[42] In his remarks Steele stressed how visual images were far more effective than words in their ability to impress ideas of Virtue and Humanity on the mind, and he praised Raphael's Cartoons as "an exercise in the highest piety of the painter." Steele was very politic in urging subscriptions,

39. Vertue (I, 50–51, 56–57; III, 8) is disappointingly sketchy about how the invitation was extended. Walpole (1763, 108–9), who drew on Vertue's notes (and on Dorigny's account of his own life as told to Vertue), gives a more coherent account of those events but not much additional information.

40. Letters written by John Talman in the spring of 1708/9 before he left for Italy and in the autumn of 1709, by which time he had arrived in Florence, suggest that he may well have been the person who urged Dorigny to England. Talman spent some twenty of his forty-nine years in foreign travel, during which time he not only formed a remarkable collection of prints and drawings but also acquired works for patrons at home and oversaw engraving projects.

In a letter dated 24 March 1708/9 to the highly esteemed virtuoso and fellow of All Souls George Clarke, Talman discussed the opportunity to be of service to Dean Aldrich of Christ Church. Apparently he was referring to a commission to copy Raphael's frescoes in the Stanza della Segnatura, and Talman made some additional suggestions, noting that "Designs made after this manner would amply compensate for their charge, and may remain lasting monuments of Rafael when the original walls shall be no more." He then requested that letters be sent to some worthy person in Rome, "for the Pope having forbid painters coming to the Vatican it will not be easy to bring these matters about." The letter ends with an offer to have the dean's fine views of Christ Church etched by an eminent person now in Rome.

Other letters from Talman in Italy, as one to Mr. Topham of 18 November 1709, indicate that on arrival he swiftly recommended himself to oversee a challenging project to copy and engrave a complete corpus of antiquities, statues, gems, etc., beginning in Florence, with the reminder that it "would require both time and money and a person to overlook such a work who would be not only skillful but diligent and faithful." He further suggested that "the best method would seem to be an allowance from the crown, which would be an honour to our kingdom." Both the plan and the phrasing run remarkably close to the proposal for the engraving of the Cartoons (Bodleian Library, MS. Eng. Letters e.34 [1708–12]).

41. W. H. Pyne, *The History of the Royal Residences, Windsor Castle,* St. James's . . . , 1819, 2:84, remarked that Queen Anne commiserated his embarrassment.

42. No. 226, 19 November 1711. Rev. W. Gunn, *Cartonensia or, an Historical and Critical Account of the Tapestries in the Palace of the Vatican,* London, 1831, 25.

mindful of sponsoring the efforts not simply of a foreign artist but of a French one at that. With verbal agility he recommended the project, noting, "It is certainly the greatest honor we can do our Country, to distinguish Strangers of Merit who apply to us with Modesty and Diffidence, which generally accompanies Merit." Steele's use of the word "Strangers" avoided identifying Dorigny as French, while his use of the epithets "Modesty and Diffidence" almost obviated that possibility—at least for an Englishman.

In the spring of 1712 Dorigny began preparing all the drawings himself and then sent to Paris for two engravers to assist him, Charles Dupuis and Claude Dubosc. After two or three years, however, some contention apparently developed between Dorigny and his assistants, and with the plates only about half completed Dupuis returned to Paris while Dubosc remained in London to take on various engraving projects for booksellers.[43] Dorigny finished the plates on his own, and in April 1719 he presented copies of his folio edition *Pinacotheca Hamptoniana* (figs. 12, 16) to George I and to the Prince and Princess of Wales. He was rewarded with a purse of a hundred guineas from the king, a gold medal from the prince, forgiveness of the interest on a four-hundred pound loan from the duke of Devonshire, and a knighthood procured for him by the duke in 1720.[44]

Dorigny's set of engravings became a print collector's staple and is to be found among the listings of most eighteenth-century sale catalogues of serious print collections.[45] The lettering on these prints is exclusively in Latin, which underscores the educated market at which they were aimed. In technical proficiency these large-scale prints vied favorably with earlier French and Italian offerings (figs. 13, 17, 34),[46] while advertising a formidable artistic treasure in the possession of the English Crown.

This latest set of Raphael prints still seems to have failed to satisfy a demanding connoisseur like Richardson. He thought they were very poor, dismissing them as works "engraved with assistance in his old age," adding that there was nothing Dorigny did after his stellar performance on the the *Transfiguration* that was worth preserving.[47] Indeed, Richardson was critical even before the prints were engraved. When he watched Dorigny make drawings in the Cartoon Gallery at Hampton Court, Richardson "looking upon his drawings shrugd up his shoulders & cryd poor Raphael! poor Raphael!"[48] On the other hand, when the painter Hans Hysing saw Richardson's own drawings traced from the Cartoons, he called them "miserable poor stuff in comparison of those of Dorignys."[49] Richardson disarmed his critics by readily admitting that his drawings were not so well handled as Dorigny's but claimed that he had accomplished the more important task of better preserving the character of

43. Walpole 1763, 111.

44. Vertue III, 11. In "From Marcantonio Raimondi to the Postcard," E. Miller notes that Dorigny was the first of only two individuals in the history of British art to be knighted for having made particular prints.

45. Thornhill Sale B included at least three sets of Dorigny's Cartoons, among them one set of off-tracts, or counterproofs, which are impressions taken from prints showing the image oriented as on the engraved plate.

46. Giovanni Battista Franco's engraving of *The Lame Man Healed* probably was after a preliminary drawing by Raphael rather than after the tapestry, and Marcantonio Raimondi's *Parnassus* is after a first sketch rather than after the fresco.

47. Richardson 1792, 263.

48. Vertue III, 13. As Vertue recounts the story, Dorigny, not proficient in English and somewhat deaf, was not quite sure of Richardson's meaning. When he finally understood, he offered Richardson his pencil so that Richardson could show him his faults, but Richardson apparently declined the challenge.

49. Ibid.

Raphael.[50] With his eyesight failing, Dorigny returned to France in April 1724, having sold at auction on 21 February 1722/3 the off-tracts of some 104 heads, hands, and feet that he made from the Cartoons.[51]

COMPETITORS

After severing ties with Dorigny, Claude Dubosc (1682–ca.1745) lost no time going into competition with him. He probably aimed to benefit from the demand for Dorigny's prints, and perhaps to undercut the price as well, when he offered printsellers a slightly smaller-size set of engravings in 1721 under the imprint of both John Bowles and William Tegg.[52] Vertue even implied that there was some underhanded agreement between Dubosc and Bowles.[53] Dubosc engraved only three of the plates himself and, in need of assistance, engaged Nicholas Beauvais and Bernard Lépicié to do the other four.[54] Dubosc seems to have been involved in numerous commercial ventures, making English versions of prints issued earlier in Paris[55] as well as undertaking the re-engraving of works published in Amsterdam.[56]

Richard Dalton (ca.1715–91), whom Ellis Waterhouse describes as "failed painter, antiquarian draughtsman, artistic busybody and engraver,"[57] was another man who well appreciated the commercial success of Dorigny's engravings and who hoped to take advantage of a market opportunity. Dalton's plan was to extend the project by making drawings from tapestries in the Vatican that were executed after twelve *other* cartoons (now lost) by Raphael. Accordingly, he went to Rome, where, under the protection of Cardinal Valenti, secretary of state, he received permission to have the tapestries hung in the apartments of the Vatican for as long as he needed. When the drawings were completed, Dalton tried to raise funds for engraving the plates by offering subscriptions, and in 1752 he printed a pamphlet describing his intentions.[58] Some thirty years later, in 1781, the project was still not completed, and Dalton published yet another pamphlet, but this time it was an apology and explanation.[59]

50. Ibid. When assessing engravings after Raphael, Richardson preferred the work of Marcantonio Raimondi; for although he believed it fell far short of what Raphael had done, all others were vastly short of him, "because he has better imitated what is most excellent in that beloved, wonderful man than any other has done" (Richardson 1773, 234–35).

51. While there are contemporary references to this sale, it is not listed in Lugt, and I have been unable to locate a copy of the catalogue. According to Vertue, Charles Jervas bought the drawings after the Cartoons that Dorigny had made for engraving his plates. Dorigny apparently had lost an opportunity to sell them earlier for several hundred pounds, and Jervas acquired them for the bargain price of forty guineas (Vertue III, 103). Dorigny died in Paris in 1746, twenty-two years after his return. Regarding off-tracts, see n. 45 and 117.

52. In-folio *en largeur*, eight plates, in reverse, with a title page with a portrait of Raphael after Paul Pontius, engraved by Nicolas Tardieu, and with a dedication to William and Mary.

53. Vertue IV, 187.

54. Ibid., 188. Nicholas Dauphin de Beauvais (1687–1763) was the son-in-law of Gaspard Duchange, who frequently imported engravings from Holland and England and who was Dubosc's representative at Paris (M. Préaud et al., *Dictionnaire des éditeurs d'estampes à Paris sous l'ancien régime*, Paris, 1987, 112).

55. Walpole 1763, 111. On 15 October 1734, a box of prints was confiscated which had been sent from London to the Abbé Bignon, who was head of the book publishers' trade in Paris. Of these prints, fifteen were copied after the Watteau prints published in Paris between 1727 and 1731 and were chiefly engraved and sold in London by Dubosc (P. Fuhring, "The Print Privilege in Eighteenth-Century France," *Print Quarterly*, II, September 1985, 185).

56. Vertue III, 67. Dubosc undertook to publish in English, by weekly subscription, *The Religious Ceremonies of all Nations*, issued in 1733 by Mons. Picart in Amsterdam.

57. E. Waterhouse, *The Dictionary of Eighteenth-Century Painters*, London, 1981, 99.

58. *Remarks on XII Historical Designs of Raphael, and the Musaeum Graeum et Aegyptiacum, or Antiquities of Greece and Egypt; illustrated by Prints, Intended to be published from Mr. Dalton's drawings. In answer to a letter of Inquiry concerning those works.*

59. Gunn, *Cartonensia*, 28–29.

OTHER COPYISTS

Following their acquisition by Charles I in the 1620s, the Cartoons were copied for a variety of ends. The earliest examples are those painted by Thomas de Critz, René Feuilliet, and Francis Cleyn (or his studio).[60] Typically, these copies were made to assist the production of tapestries at Mortlake (e.g., see fig. 10), where a manufactory had been set up by James I in 1619.[61] Prompted by the example of the Hampton Court display, some of these replicas would eventually line drawing rooms of country houses. The painted copies by Francis Cleyn were put on display by the sixth earl of Dorset in his own Cartoon Gallery at Knole in Kent in 1701, just two years after the originals were installed at the royal palace.[62] Of course, tapestries were more plentiful, and in the eighteenth century either sets or individual pieces (often cut to straddle fireplaces and doors) were to be seen at Althorp, Boughton, Belvoir Castle, Chatsworth, Ford-Abbey, Longleat, Petworth, and Wilton.[63]

In addition to painted copies, numerous drawings were made directly from the Cartoons, first by Gribelin and then by Dorigny as part of the elaborate process required for engraving their plates. But a number of other artists were also granted access to Hampton Court, each with a somewhat different motive. Jonathan Richardson was surely impelled by a desire to improve his connoisseur's eye. Although none of his drawings after the Cartoons can be identified,[64] he was known as one of Raphael's most attentive observers and can readily be imagined on the scaffold with other Raphael drawings in hand, probing for nuances of style and plying his rational, empirical method—the very practice he recommended for refining critical judgment.

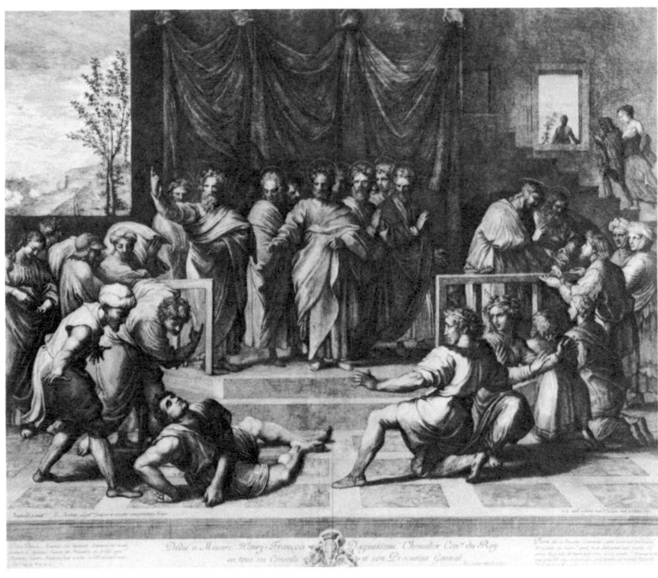

FIG. 18 Gérard Audran (after Charles Jervas, after Raphael), *The Death of Ananias,* ca.1702–3 (*cat. 1*)

60. Vertue I, 68–69; Croft-Murray, 1:195, 201, 247.

61. In 1637 it became the Royal Manufactory.

62. St. J. Gore, "The Paintings of the Early Sackvilles; The Collection at Knole–I," *Country Life,* 7 October 1965, 886–88. Also see *The National Trust Guidebook to Knole,* 1989.

63. See S. Markham, *John Lovday of Caversham 1711–1789,* London, 1984, 99, 193, 201, 238, 294, 344, and Marillier, MS. Notes. One of the tapestries at Longleat, *Elymas the Sorcerer Struck with Blindness,* inspired a lengthy poetic tribute by A. Finch (Chadwyck-Healy, English Poetry Full-Text Database [EPFTD], 1994).

64. See p. 29.

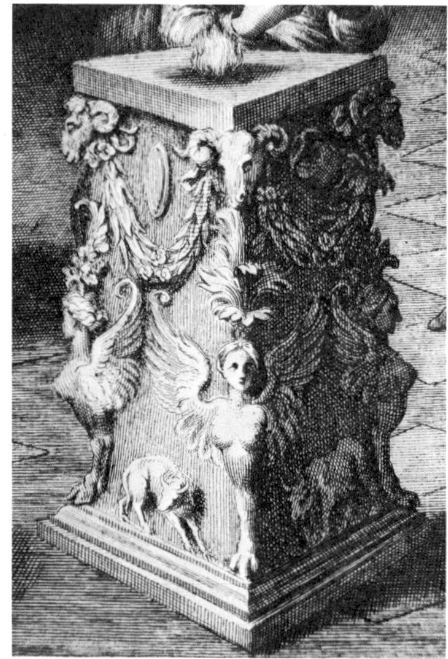

FIG. 19 Gérard Audran (after Raphael), *Paul and Barnabas at Lystra*, detail, ca.1702–3, etching and engraving, Victoria and Albert Museum

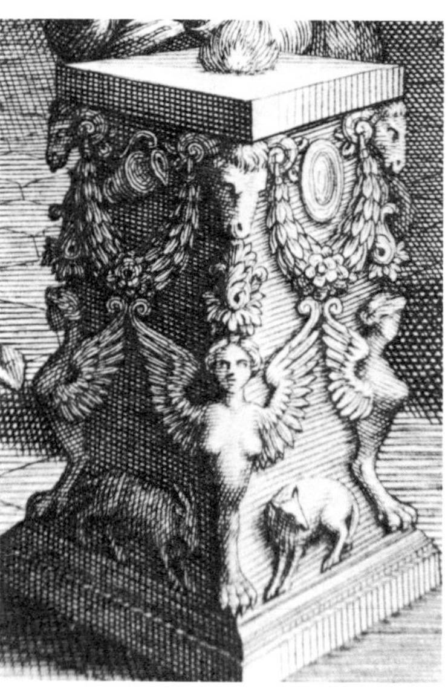

FIG. 20 Simon Gribelin (after Raphael), *Paul and Barnabas at Lystra*, detail (1707), 1720 (*cat. 9f*)

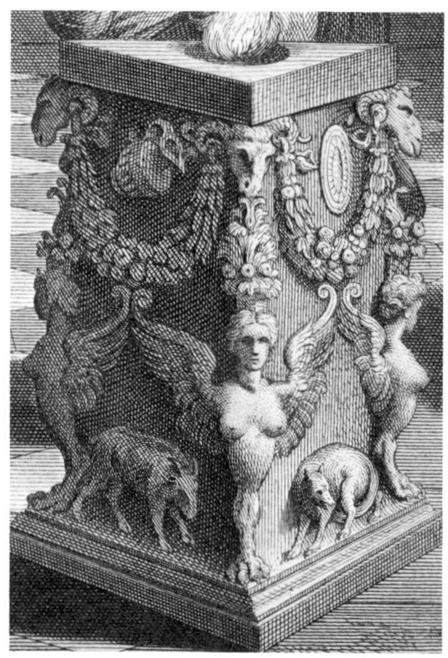

FIG. 21 Nicolas Dorigny (after Raphael), *Paul and Barnabas at Lystra*, detail, 1719 (*cat. 4f*)

Charles Jervas (1675–1739),[65] the Irish painter whom Alexander Pope considered *Raphael Secundus*, also made copies of the Cartoons. This would have been around 1698, just a few years after Jervas had been a pupil of Godfrey Kneller, when he had easy access to Hampton Court because of his friendship with a Mr. Norrice, the keeper of pictures and frame maker to the Crown.[66] That opportunity was apparently of little benefit, for later in his career he complained that by copying the Cartoons so early in his training he had learned the art of painting at the wrong end–claiming that he did not learn to draw until he went to Rome, around 1703.[67]

We learn from Vertue that one set of Jervas's copies was "about half len. Cloths." and was bought by the artist's great friend and patron Dr. George Clarke of All Souls, Oxford.[68] It was from these copies that Gérard Audran, whose graphic style was applauded for capturing the painterly qualities of the originals, made two engravings of the Cartoons (fig. 18; compare engraving styles in figs. 19, 20, 21). Jervas had made the arrangements with Audran

65. For a profile of Jervas, see A. Crookshank and The Knight of Glin, *The Painters of Ireland ca.1660–1920*, London, 1979, 34–35.

66. Vertue III, 15, 42. The Cartoons were available for copying a few years prior to their official installation. Christopher Hatton wrote to his brother, Viscount Hatton, on 2 September 1697, "I have this day, my lord, been at Hampton Court but ye sight best pleased me was ye cartoons by Raphael which are far beyond all ye paintings I ever saw. They are brought from ye tower and hung up there and are copying for my Lord Sunderland" (*Wren Society*, VII, 197). A letter by William Talman of 12 September 1699 more precisely dates their installation–"the gallery for the Cartoones of Raphell is so forward that I shall fix up the pictures in a week" (British Library, Add. MSS. 20,101 f.69).

67. Ibid., 16. It was probably Kneller who prompted Jervas to copy the Cartoons, since his own training in Rome had entailed copying Raphael's paintings in the Vatican (J. D. Stewart, *Sir Godfrey Kneller and the English Baroque Portrait*, Oxford, 1983, 7).

68. Vertue III, 42. I assume that by "half len. Cloth." Vertue refers to canvas of the standard half-length portrait format of 36 by 28 inches (the three-quarter format typically was 50 by 40 inches, and the full-length 90 by 60 inches).

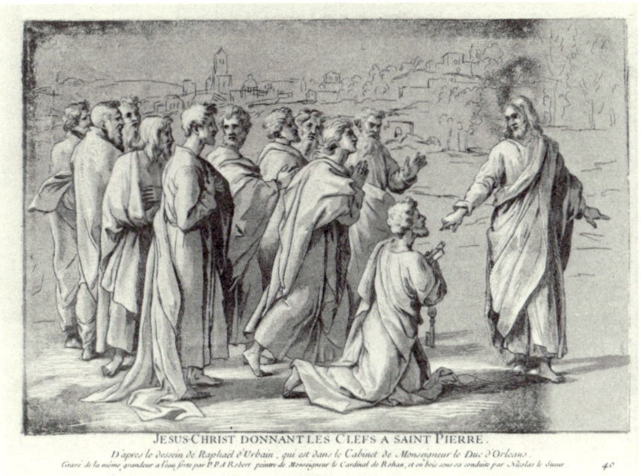

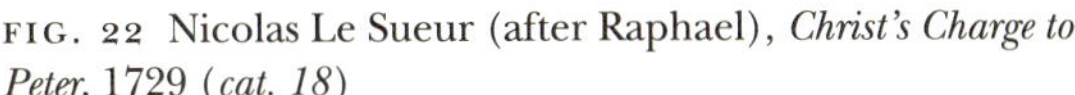

FIG. 22 Nicolas Le Sueur (after Raphael), *Christ's Charge to Peter*, 1729 (*cat. 18*)

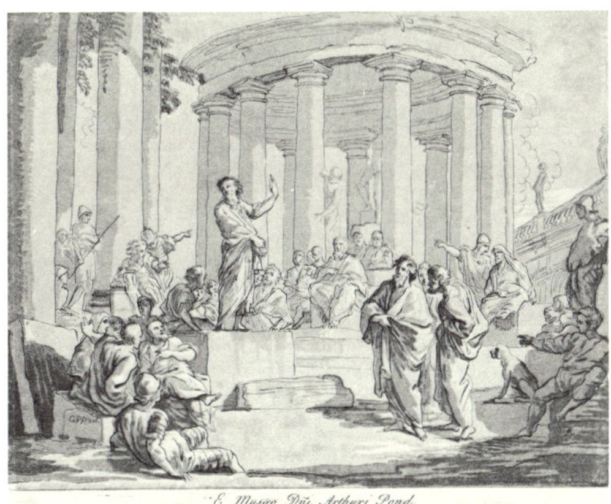

FIG. 23 Arthur Pond and Charles Knapton (after Panini), *Paul Preaching at Athens*, 1736 (*cat. 20*)

when he stopped in Paris on route to Italy, and Clarke, a prodigious collector of prints who probably initiated the project, had the paintings sent to Paris.[69] In addition to these copies made for Clarke, three other sets surfaced in the sale that followed Jervas's death in 1739.[70] These additional sets were probably not the labors of his early training but more likely date from sometime after 1732, the year he lost the King's favor, having painted a disappointing likeness of George II into John Wootton's large equestrian portrait. Although Jervas had been principal painter to the King since 1723, from then on he spent his time making the many copies after old masters that one finds listed for disposal at his posthumous sale.[71]

When Christopher Le Blon (1667–1741) copied the Cartoons in 1729, it was as in the earliest days with a commercial eye to the manufacture of tapestries. He was granted a warrant by the king to loom sets of tapestries by an entirely new method of his own devising. Le Blon had previously experimented with full-color printing, and now he attempted to apply some of that experience to the tapestry-weaving process. He promised that his process would be far less costly than any in existence, and that he could produce sets of tapestries at £100, that is, at one tenth the current price. The novelty of his method was that the patterns were drawn in a way that would allow any common draft-weaver to mount the loom: paintings on paper would be overprinted with a copper plate engraved with a grid whose subdivisions corresponded to the threads of the warp.[72] Alas, this most ingenious scheme never materialized; such was the fate of many of what Vertue called Le Blon's "delusional" commercial ventures.[73]

69. Ibid., 15–16, 42. Audran died in 1703, having engraved only two of the seven Cartoons. For an excellent discussion of Clarke's print collecting activities, see T. Clayton, "The Print Collection of George Clarke at Worcester College, Oxford," *Print Quarterly*, IX, 1992, 123–37 (with thanks to E. Miller for calling my attention to this article).

70. Charles Jervas's collection was sold 11–20 March 1739/40 (Lugt 498). Listed are the following sets: March 12 (105) The Seven Cartoons from Raphael, by Jarvis, 54 by 81 inches, £30.10s; March 15 (319) The Cartoons from Raphael by C. Jarvis, 58 inches (no width nor sale price recorded); March 17 (392) The Seven Cartoons from Raphael by C. Jarvis, 40 by 55 inches (no price recorded). Many items from Jervas's sale resurfaced in the sale of Mr. John Hampden 1–3 April 1754 (Lugt 831), and among them are The Seven Cartoons by Jarvis (lot 67, no size given). From Dorigny's sale in February 1723 Jervas bought the drawings Dorigny made for engraving the Cartoons.

71. Whitley, 1:44–45.

72. "An Account of Mr. James Christopher Le Blon's Principles of Printing, in Imitation of Painting, and of Weaving Tapestry, in the same manner as Brocades," *Philosophical Transactions of the Royal Society*, 1731, no. 419, 101 (reprinted in VII, 1809, 477–80).

73. Vertue (III, 62, 69, 99) commented at length on Le Blon's

In the 1730s, when it became fashionable to reproduce drawings as prints, and in a variety of tonal techniques, Nicolas Le Sueur produced a stunning chiaroscuro wood engraving after a drawing related to the Cartoon of *Christ's Charge to Peter* (fig. 22). It was published in the influential *Cabinet de Crozat* (1729)[74]–which reproduced old-master drawings from major French collections–a work that probably induced Arthur Pond and Charles Knapton to undertake the reproduction of master drawings from outstanding English collections. Their *Prints in Imitation of Drawings* (1736)[75] aimed to undermine the French domination of the market for quality reproductions of old-master works. Included in their compendium, conceivably as a counterpart to Le Sueur's engraving, was a print after a drawing by Panini which is a very free interpretation of Raphael's *Paul Preaching at Athens* (fig. 23).

JAMES THORNHILL AND THE CARTOONS

When Thornhill began copying the Cartoons at Hampton Court in 1729, Vertue voiced regret at the sorry state of affairs "that after so much reputation. friends & meritt. as the most Excellent Native history painter . . . he hath not great work, or imployment underhand."[76] Vertue's lament that Thornhill's reputation and commissions diminished in the mid-1720s does not, however, justify the recent conclusion that Thornhill was "reduced to copying."[77] After all, he lived under no financial pressures.[78] Still, one may well ask why England's foremost history painter–who received prestigious sacred and secular decorative commissions, was sergeant painter to the king (1718–32), and was the first native-born painter to be knighted (1720)–would spend three unpaid years making copies.

Of course, Jervas, who enjoyed a respectable reputation as a portraitist, also made many copies of the Cartoons, both in his youth as an exercise in learning his craft and again in his later years as a professional copyist servicing a market. But for Thornhill, copying Raphael was another matter. At this point in his life and career copying the Cartoons was certainly not a mere exercise. Around 1709 Thornhill had apparently studied the Cartoons very carefully in the course of devising his compositions for the decoration of the cupola of Saint

---

various "delusional" projects, and he seemed to take special pleasure relating that the House of Commons rejected Le Blon's petition in 1733 for a renewal of his expired patent for "Weaveing of Tapistry in the Loom."

74. What is known as the *Cabinet de Crozat* consists of two volumes of prints published under the title *Recueil d'Estampes d'après les plus beaux tableaux et d'après les plus beaux dessins qui sont en France dans le Cabinet du Roy, dans celuy de Monseigneur le Duc d'Orleans & dans d'autres cabinets devise suivant les differents écoles avec une abrige de la vie des peintres & une description historique de chaque tableau*, Paris, 1729 and 1742. This formidable undertaking, which set a high standard for reproductive engraving, was proposed by the duc d'Orleans, supported by Pierre J. Mariette, and financed by Pierre Crozat and subscribers.

75. See H. M. Hake, "Pond and Knapton's Imitation of Drawings," *Print Collector's Quarterly*, IX, 1922, 324–49.

76. Vertue III, 38.

77. *English Baroque Sketches*, exh. cat., Marble Hill House, London, 1974 (s.v. "Thornhill"). We do know that after Thornhill's work at Moor Park (1725–27) no commissions were forthcoming; by the 1730s commissions for the type of painting that was Thornhill's forte were increasingly scarce. Around that same time, Francis Hayman (who recently had completed his apprenticeship with Thornhill's former assistant Robert Browne), turned to the theater for employment, because there were no opportunities in the decorative genre in which he was trained (B. Allen, *Francis Hayman*, exh. cat., Kenwood, London, 1987, 49–50).

78. Vertue III, 38, where he notes that it was "happy for him, that his fortune, is very easy."

Paul's (figs. 71–73). Moreover, he had been employed at Hampton Court painting the Prince of Wales's bedchamber in 1714, at the same time that Dorigny, a fellow director at the Great Queen Street Academy, was in residence working on drawings preparatory to engraving the Cartoons. Thus, by the time Thornhill received his own warrant in 1729 to work from the Cartoons, Raphael's Apostles must have seemed like old friends. Indeed, he perhaps took as a personal challenge the claim, made in the lavish folio volume of prints *Cabinet de Crozat* published the year he began, that engraved reproductions were superior to painted copies because the latter were usually mediocre.[79]

For Thornhill, copying Raphael was a self-appointed task; in doing so, he can be seen to have consciously positioned himself as the doyen of an incipient "British School" and to have assumed the role of aesthetic broker. In this era of economic prosperity, increased attention was focused on aesthetic concerns, and attempts to rekindle the arts—which had sadly languished since the glorious days of the Caroline Court—were linked to the larger issue of national identity. Shaftesbury reminded his countrymen that "One who aspires to the Character of a Man of Breeding and Politeness, is careful to form his Judgment of Arts and Sciences upon right Models of Perfection."[80] This concern with proper models of imitation led sculptors to a large and authoritative corpus of Greco-Roman marbles.[81] Painters, however, only had Pliny's verbal descriptions of the works of their ancient precursors. Since these were scarcely useful as guides to perfecting their craft, painters turned to the great Renaissance masters as exemplars, above all, to the paintings of Raphael as the normative models of the classical style.

In England, Jonathan Richardson's writings offered the most insistent and authoritative word on Raphael's prowess (see below pp. 46–51), while Dorigny's folio prints were the officially sanctioned replications of his compositions. Thornhill, a confident British history painter, may well have hoped to preempt the French engraver's position. Being both English and Protestant had given him the decisive edge earlier when he won out over a virtuoso market of French and Venetian decorative painters in the competition to paint the cupola of Saint Paul's.

In the end, Thornhill won critical approbation, and even Vertue—who bristled when fellow artists enjoyed what he considered unmerited acclaim, and who was always quick to voice a complaint—lauded him for having captured the true spirit and character of Raphael. The endorsement is especially striking in light of the fact that Vertue himself had copied Raphael two years earlier, engraving the *Portrait of Castiglione* for an English translation of *The Courtier* (1727).[82]

79. Regarding the *Cabinet de Crozat,* see n.74. As to the motivation for copying paintings by Raphael, there are some interesting parallels between Thornhill and Mengs. See the discussion of the circumstances surrounding Mengs's copy of Raphael's *School of Athens* by S. Roettgen, *Mengs e Raffaello: rendiconto di un rapporto programmato,* Rome, 1990, 631–34.

80. See n. 14.

81. These were not necessarily originals, but nonetheless they were well known through casts and engravings. For a comprehensive discussion of the reconstructed corpus of antiquity in the eighteenth century, see F. Haskell and N. Penny, *Taste and the Antique: The Lure of Classical Sculpture, 1500–1900,* New Haven, 1981.

82. J. Nicols, *Literary Anecdotes of the Eighteenth Century,* London, 1812, 1:709.

Vertue acknowledged that Thornhill's copies were done with all possible exactness, and noted too that Thornhill had judiciously observed and corrected the many accidents that the originals had suffered owing to time and the damage done by two-hundred years of unskilled repairs.[83] Vertue observed that Thornhill carefully drew and studied all the parts of the Cartoons, with the aim of preserving for posterity a truer idea of Raphael than conveyed hitherto, and remarked that he was better equipped to undertake this task than any man living.[84] Thornhill's obituary in *Gentleman's Magazine* also offered a positive interpretation of this preoccupation of his later years. The extravagant encomium to "the greatest History Painter this Kingdom ever produced" acknowledged the service of Thornhill's brush in reviving Raphael's rich but decayed Cartoons.[85]

THORNHILL'S COPIES: THE "SAME-SIZE" SET

Because of ambiguities in Vertue's notes, there is some uncertainty about the number of sets of copies that Thornhill made.[86] Nonetheless, absolutely bona fide is one same-size set on canvas, rendered in an oil and turpentine wash.[87] The diluted oil medium closely simulated the thin pigmentation of the gouache (distemper) originals and at the same time promised greater permanence.[88] Thornhill died just three years after the completion of these copies, and although he doubtless had some destination for them in mind, they came to be offered for sale with the rest of his collection in February 1734/5.[89] They were bought by John Russell, fourth duke of Bedford, for £200 (lot 101), a sum that Vertue remarked was less than the cost of the canvas and colors.[90] Vertue was dismayed that the labor of England's foremost history painter fetched such a paltry sum, but Walpole quite sensibly attributed the low price to the lack of bidders with houses of sufficient space to accommodate the works' display.[91] These full-scale copies hung for a number of years in a magnificent gallery at Bedford House, the elegant residence designed by Inigo Jones on the north side of Bloomsbury Square.[92] When the house was demolished and its contents sold in 1800,[93]

83. Around a hundred years later, Trull proposed that the Cartoons could best be purged of the errors introduced by restorers by comparing them with the original set of tapestries, claiming that the fame of the Apostles series rested on the tapestries and *not* on the Cartoons (W. Trull, *Raphael Vindicated; by a comparison between the original tapestries [now in London] of Leo X and the Cartoons at Hampton Court, as repaired by Cooke*, London, 1840).

84. Vertue III, 39, 43.

85. May 1734, 174–75.

86. See n. 21.

87. By "same-size" I mean sharing the same dimensions of the Cartoons, approximately 135 by 210 inches (three of the seven Cartoons, however, are narrower in width).

88. Henry Cooke (1642?–1700), who had been employed by William III to repair the Raphael Cartoons after their use at the Mortlake tapestry works, had also made copies in oil imitating distemper. Listed in the sale of his collection of pictures after his death were "many fine copies of the cartoons, drawn in turpentine oil, after the manner of distemper" (Croft-Murray, 1:245, citing Bainbrigg Buckeridge, *An Essay Towards an English-School*, London, 1706). One of Cooke's sets later hung in the Picture Gallery at Oxford. The pictures had been given to Oxford by John, duke of Marlborough, and are identified in *The Handbook Guide for the University Galleries*, Oxford, 1846, 22–23, as "colored drawings on paper." On several occasions these were incorrectly attributed to Thornhill.

89. Thornhill Sale A, 25 February, lot 101.

90. Vertue III, 70, 74.

91. Walpole IV, 47 (this first appears in the 1782 edition).

92. "Besides the body of the house, are two wings, and on each side the proper offices. One of the wings is a magnificent gallery in which are copies of the Cartoons at Hampton Court as large as the originals, by Sir James Thornhill" (*London and its Environs Described*, 1761, 1:331). Before the house became the Bedford's London seat in the early eighteenth century, it was known as Southampton House (G. Worsley, "The 'Best Turned' House of the Duke of Bedford," *The Georgian Group Journal*, VI, 1966, 63–73.

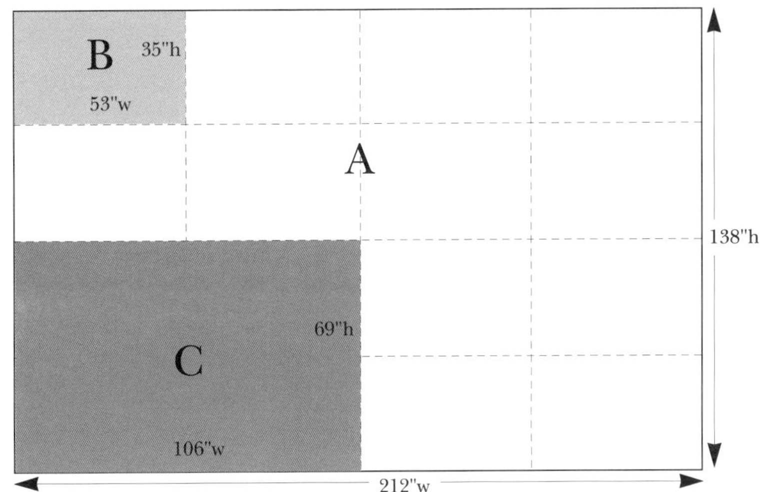

DIAGRAM 1
A= scale of Raphael's Cartoons
B= "quarter-size" (1/16 of original)
C= "half-size" (1/4 of original)

Francis Russell, the fifth duke, presented the copies to the Royal Academy, the very destination (*avant la lettre*) Thornhill probably had in mind. Since then, their whereabouts have been known; they have moved around London with the Royal Academy as it moved its quarters from the Strand to Trafalgar Square and then to Piccadilly.[94] At present they are rolled up in the basement of Burlington House, ironically in greater need of restoration than the preciously cared for originals which are now at the Victoria and Albert Museum.

THORNHILL'S COPIES: THE "QUARTER-SIZE" SET

At various points in his notebooks Vertue also referred to other sets. In August of 1729 he first mentioned a "smaller sett being one fourth of the large originals whereby these will be just every part half so big as the others," noting that these would be strengthened in color and highly finished in oil.[95] Two years later, after Thornhill had completed the full-size set, Vertue mentioned "another sett of Coppies a fourth part as big as the originals. these are also curiously Coppy'd and made all of square size."[96] One might assume that these two references were to the same set, until a later notation in 1734—made in the course of eulogizing Thornhill after his death—distinguished between two *different* scaled-down versions. There Vertue described "one sett made by him of half the magnitude. & an other of a fourth part of the originals."[97] In this latest description, however, Vertue used the terms *half-size* and *quarter-size* to signify the vertical reduction of the figures and not to indicate the reduction as a percentage of the whole. This confusion in his use of terms can be clarified by taking

93. They were offered in the duke of Bedford's sale at Christies, 7 May 1800, but were probably bought in.

94. The Royal Academy was at Somerset House from 1800 until 1836, when it moved to Trafalgar Square; in 1869 it moved to its present location at Burlington House.

95. Vertue III, 39.

96. Ibid., 53.

97. Ibid., 70. Thornhill's obituary in *Gentleman's Magazine*, 1734, 174–75, referred to the Cartoons "reviv'd by his curious Pencil" and to his copies "not only in their full Proportions, but in many other sizes and shapes."

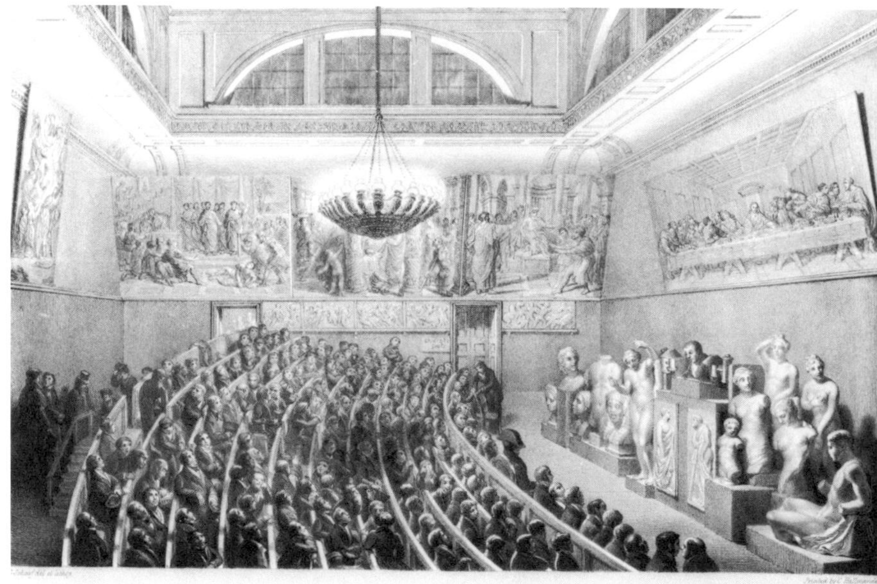

FIG. 24 George Scharf, *Lecture on Sculpture by Sir Richard Westmacott, at the Royal Academy, Somerset House, 1830*, 1836 (*cat. 27*)

into account the actual dimensions of one small-size set[98] that was also listed in Thornhill's sale.[99] This set, which was sold to an unknown buyer for seventy-five guineas, had "fine gold frames" and measured 43 1/2 by 55 inches. Stated in relation to the originals, this is actually one sixteenth—not one quarter—of their size (see diagram 1). It is quarter-size in relation to the vertical reduction, but this is not the meaning Vertue gave the term initially. By this revised definition, the half-size set would measure about 69 by 106 inches, the size of the Columbia University copies. This half-size set did not appear in Thornhill's sale, and its subsequent history is uncertain. Neither of these sets appears to fit Vertue's description of squared proportions. Nevertheless, given Vertue's frequent imprecision, that reference is most likely to the smallest of the sets, which, at least in relation to the larger and to the full-size copies, is decidedly squarish. Its height-to-width proportions are in the ratio of 4:5, a substantial departure from the 2:3 ratio of the originals.

Over the years, various copies of the Tapestry Cartoons have surfaced in auction catalogues, often without mention of size and without attribution. Healthy skepticism is called for when assessing sale catalogue claims; for example, the listing in 1832 of a set by Sir James Thornhill the same size as the originals[100] is surely bogus, since his only full-size set was then at Somerset House, home of the Royal Academy (fig. 24).

In regard to the smallest set, we learn from Vertue that in these paintings Thornhill wanted to restore the Cartoons to their original state, before their subsequent losses and repairs, taking the liberty "to add the parts or Capitals that was Cutt off. & some parts at the

98. Vertue III, 74.

99. Thornhill Sale A, 24 February, lot 98.

100. The property of George Gillows, deceased, sold by the auctioneer Stanley in London 12–13 June 1832 (109). This may well be the same set that some years earlier sold at Christies, 8 April 1774 (58), but without the Thornhill attribution.

ends as he can demonstrate was discovered by him to be done. to fitt them to the places intended when they were repaird or joynd together in K. Williams reign. by Mr. Cooke. painter."[101] After these paintings sold for seventy-five guineas at Thornhill's sale in 1735 they dropped from sight. They may have been the copies offered for sale at Jeffrey's Gallery in Salisbury in 1809, which at the time were identified as the small set mentioned by Walpole.[102] Their 40 by 50 inches tally with Vertue's notion of a "squared" format, but nothing more of this set or its ownership is known.[103] Recently, two paintings of the same dimensions were acquired for Spencer House – *The Death of Ananias* and *The Lame Man Healed* – and are presumed to have belonged to this set.[104] The difficulty is in gauging what lies beneath the recent restoration of these pictures. As they now appear, the figures have a soft and somewhat flaccid quality which, coupled with the indistinct rendering of hands, feet, and heads, seems unconvincing, especially in light of Thornhill's hundreds of painstaking preliminary studies. Charles Jervas also painted a set of similar dimensions (40 by 55 inches) whose whereabouts is not known.[105]

In view of the foregoing evidence, it seems reasonable to conclude that Thornhill probably painted three sets of copies of Raphael's Cartoons: the full-size set now at the Royal Academy; a quarter-size set whose location is uncertain, but which was listed as lot 98 in Thornhill's sale; and a half-size set that has found a home at Columbia University. The paint-

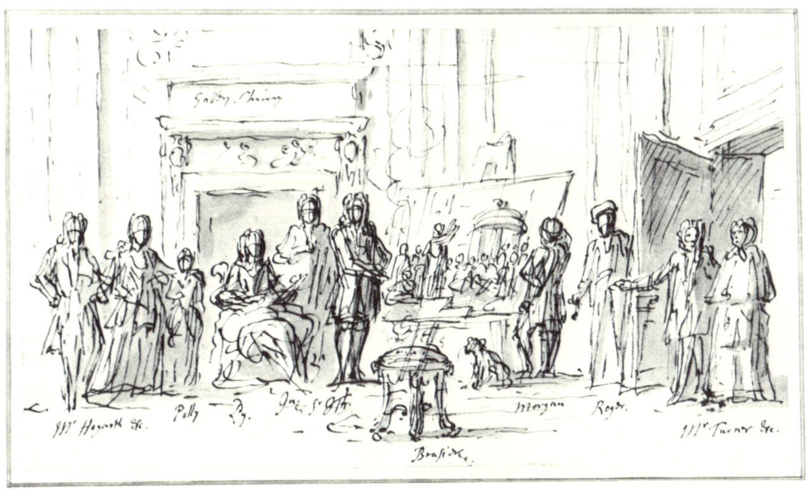

FIG. 25 James Thornhill, *Study for a Group Portrait of the Artist and His Family*, ca.1730 (*cat. 39*)

101. Vertue III, 43. The reference here is to the Cartoon of *The Lame Man Healed* in which the three large columns in the foreground do not include capitals.

102. Walpole IV, 22–23. Many thanks to Burton Fredericksen, director of the Provenance Index at the Getty Art History Information Program, for calling this sale, and innumerable other nineteenth-century sales, to my attention.

103. It is impossible to determine if these are the same as the "admirable set of cartoons, painted by Sir James Thornhill . . . very fine and accurate copies," sold by Messrs. Robbins, 19 May 1810 (94), from the collection of William Webber, Esq. of Blackheath and formerly of Duke Street. No sizes are given, but the low sale price of £63 suggests that these may have been even smaller copies and, despite the claim, perhaps by somebody else.

104. They were purchased by Lord Rothschild about 1990 from Christopher Gibbs, who contends they probably belong to Thornhill's smallest set. The addition of capitals to the columns in the latter composition is no warranty that the painting is by Thornhill (see n. 101), for it should be noted that as early as 1707 Gribelin had also vertically extended that same composition with the addition of capitals and a frieze of swags and bucranea.

105. See n. 70.

ing *Paul Preaching at Athens* from this latter set can be identified on the easel in Thornhill's sketch of himself together with family and friends (frontispiece, fig. 25).

THORNHILL'S COPIES: THE "HALF-SIZE" SET (THE COLUMBIA COPIES)

A brief prelude to the discussion of the half-size set, and more generally to the account of Thornhill's role as Raphael's factor in England, is the more recent story of how Thornhill's paintings arrived on Morningside Heights in 1959. Much like the tapestries which came to the Cathedral of Saint John the Divine in 1954, Thornhill's paintings were part of an abundant transfer of goods from England to America in the aftermath of World War I. With the wholesale demolition of country houses and the breakup of numerous estates,[106] the fittings stripped from many English interiors found an avid market and welcome walls in the United States.[107] This was also a period when the field of interior design was elevated and transformed,[108] when interest moved beyond the fabric swatch to the architectural setting. And it was under the auspices of "interior decorators"–not picture dealers–that the Thornhill paintings first surfaced in New York in the 1920s. Curiously, Thornhill's path to New York had been paved by the demolition of his own London residence at 75 Dean Street in 1921, whereupon all the fittings–staircase, walls, moldings, fireplaces, and frescos–were offered for sale at W. & J. Sloane's on Fifth Avenue, a store featuring continental furnishings for the American home.[109]

Although it has long been assumed that the set of half-size copies now at Columbia was painted by Thornhill, this exhibition provides not only the occasion to examine their claimed provenance (which unlike that of the full-scale copies, is not well documented) but also the opportunity to consider the visual evidence afforded by the paintings themselves and by the drawings that are associated with them.

When the paintings were given to the university in 1959, Rudolph Wittkower apparently expressed no doubts about either their avowed authorship or their provenance. I suspect that he would have been pleased to have any genuine eighteenth-century copies of such important works hang in the department, and I therefore doubt that he spent much time worrying whether they were unequivocally by Thornhill. Very much in their favor was that they were a gift from a knowledgeable source–Jeannette Lenygon, the widow of Francis Henry Lenygon (d. 1943), a well-known authority on English interior design whose expertise gave him a hand in the decoration of Windsor and Buckingham palaces. Mrs. Lenygon had formidable connoisseurship and art market credentials of her own: she was chairman of the

106. R. Strong, M. Binney, J. Harris, *The Destruction of the English Country House, 1875–1975*, London, 1974, 16.

107. It was an era of country house fever *avant la lettre*, an Englishing of America before the era of Ralph Lauren. The cult of the historic country house is said to have begun with the publication of J. Nash's *Mansions of England in the Olden Time*, London, 1839 (R. Strong, *Lost Treasures of Britain*, London, 1990, 127).

108. The craftsmanly designation of "upholsterer" was replaced with the more edifying title of "decorator" and a new breed of professionals emerged. Magazines such as *The Upholster* were superseded by *Interiors* and by *Interior Design*.

109. W. & J. Sloane, *Fittings of a Famous English House Known as Hogarth's House*, New York, 1921. Thornhill's house came to be known as "Hogarth's House," as it was believed to have been the dowry of his daughter Jane, who married William Hogarth in 1729.

National Committee on Historic Restoration of the American Institute of Interior Design; consultant on the furnishings at Gracie Mansion, Blair House, and the White House; and, with her husband, an adviser on the restoration of Colonial Williamsburg in the 1930s.

Shortly after the end of World War I, Mrs. Lenygon (then Jeannette Becker) had been hired by the New York office of the British firm Lenygon and Morant, Ltd., a company that sold antique furniture of high quality and historical importance.[110] The firm acquired the paintings in the United States in 1926, and they were valued in that year's inventory at $40,000,[111] a sum far in excess of any other item in the company's stock. The seven paintings now at Columbia—with their elaborate period frames – came under the aegis of "furnishings," as did the paneling and tapestries from English interiors that Lenygon and Morant offered for sale. It is probably because these pictures were sold through dealers in the decorative arts, rather than at painting auctions, that they have proved difficult to track.

The Thornhill paintings were said by Mrs. Lenygon to have formerly hung at Kirby Hall, a house in Yorkshire that was demolished in the early 1920s.[112] Although I can find no record of the contents of Kirby Hall nor of how the paintings came to the United States, unpublished reminiscences of the Dowager Lady Meysey-Thompson,[113] mother of the first and last Lord Knaresborough who sold Kirby in 1919, mention a set of copies of the Raphael Cartoons by Thornhill that came to Kirby from the duke of Chandos's house at Carmons [*sic*] which was pulled down at the time.[114]

James Brydges, first duke of Chandos, built Canons between 1713 and 1725 and employed Thornhill there for large-scale decorative work. Although there is no record of Thornhill's copies in the extensive inventory of pictures taken when Canons was demolished in 1747, other copies of the Cartoons were offered at the Canons sale (8 May 1747 [160]). But Columbia's large oil paintings could scarcely have been confused with the "8 Cartons in Water Colours after those of Hampton Court by Raphael Urbin—by Jo. Goupy."[115] Joseph Goupy, who is best known for small gouache copies after old-master paint-

110. In 1915 Francis Lenygon entered into partnership with the upholsterer Morant, and also secured the services of the furniture expert Margaret Jourdain, who prepared the texts of books on the history of furniture and decoration that appeared under Lenygon's name (see Lenygon and Morant, Ltd., holdings, National Art Library, London).

111. Lenygon Papers, Avery Architectural and Fine Arts Library, Inventory Books, no. 4607.

112. Kirby Hall, Yorkshire, was designed by Richard Boyle, third earl of Burlington, and Robert Morris for Stephen Thompson ca.1747–55 and executed by the architect John Carr. The house should not be confused with another Kirby Hall in Northamptonshire, which by 1825 had fallen into ruin after it was deserted by its owners, the Finch-Hattons.

113. Née Elizabeth Anne Croft (1818–1910), widow of Sir Harry Stephen Meysey-Thompson. This information is from the Royal Commission on Historical Monuments, and I thank Brian D. Mitchell for tracking down this evidence of the Thornhill paintings at Kirby Hall, as well as for a reference in *Country Life* (17 February 1972, 388) mentioning that the vanished Kirby Hall "is supposed to have incorporated work by Grinling Gibbons and paintings by Thornhill that had come from Canons."

114. Mrs. Lenygon claimed that for a long time the paintings were in the possession of the duke of Chandos, whom she identified as a patron of Robert Adam. This would have been James Brydges, the third duke (1771–89), for whom Adam designed Chandos House, Portland Place, in 1770–71. If correct, this would suggest that the paintings did not go directly to Kirby when Canons was demolished (as the "reminiscences" imply) but some time later. It seems more likely, however, that Mrs. Lenygon confused the first and the third dukes.

115. Vertue III, 136. The Duke had paid more than £300, but they sold for only £17.6s.

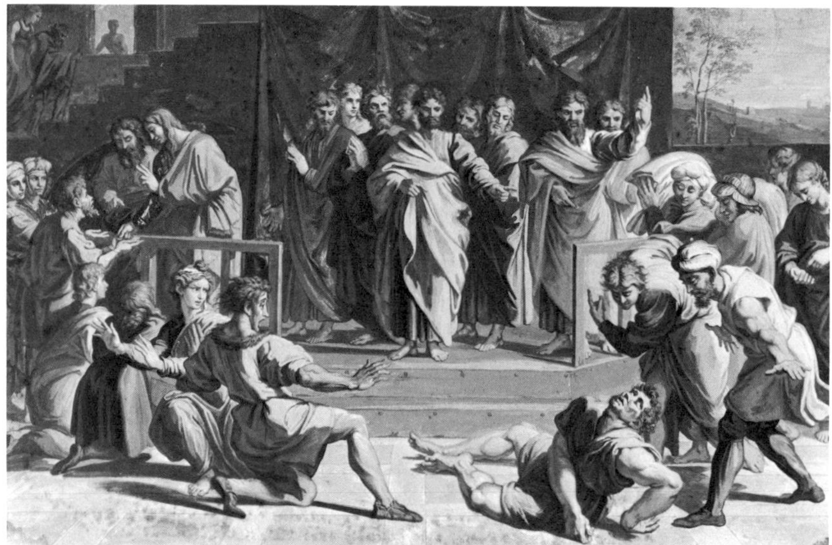

FIG. 26 Joseph Goupy (after Raphael), *The Death of Ananias*, ca.1717, gouache on parchment, 11 7/8 by 18 inches, Yale Center for British Art, Paul Mellon Collection

ings,[116] made several small-scale copies of the Raphael Cartoons (fig. 26),[117] among them the set at Canons which was on parchment[118] and a somewhat smaller set at Knowsley Hall, painted in bodycolour directly over Dorigny's engravings.

It is of note that while Thornhill was employed painting the staircase and saloon at Canons (1719–24), the duke of Chandos bought a set of four "Creation" cartoons, purportedly by Raphael but of doubtful authenticity.[119] As it turned out, the saloon at Canons was too small for these cartoons,[120] and one can speculate that from the start the half-size copies Thornhill painted—a few years after the fiasco of the duke's purchase of the bogus Raphaels—were earmarked for that room. If this speculation is correct, Columbia's half-size set did not appear in the Thornhill sale of February 1734/5 (unlike the full-size and quarter-size sets), because it was already the property of the duke of Chandos for whom it had been painted.

Although the paintings seem to have gone unrecorded while at Canons, and were only

116. Goupy was a drawing teacher who also held an appointment as cabinet painter to Frederick, Prince of Wales. See J. Simon, "New Light on Joseph Goupy (1689–1769)," *Apollo*, February 1994, 15-18, and B. Robertson, "Joseph Goupy and the Art of the Copy," *Bulletin of the Cleveland Museum of Art*, LXXV, no. 10, December 1988, 355–83.

117. G. Scharf describes a set recorded at Knowsley Hall in 1736, painted by Goupy in bodycolour with print lines seen under the painting in several parts, the same size as Dorigny's originals and the same color as the Cartoons but paler; as these are in reverse of the engravings, they are off-tracks (*Catalogue of the Collection of Pictures at Knowsley Hall*, London, 1875, 467–74).

118. The provenance given for these paintings in *The Quiet Conquest: The Huguenots 1685 to 1985*, exh. cat., Museum of London, 1985 [291], confuses two different sets of copies: one that Goupy painted for his patron Baron Kielmansegg, for which he was paid 220 guineas and which then passed to the duke of Chandos; and another set that belonged to the Prince of Wales, which Vertue saw in the Princess's dressing room at Leicester House in 1749 (Vertue III, 152). In addition, a set was listed in the sale of John Huggins's collection in 1745 (2nd day, lot 135), and a set was recorded at Knowsley Hall in 1736.

119. He bought them abroad, via Henry Davenant. For the story of the purchase, restoration, and attempts to dispose of these "Creation" cartoons, see C. H. Collins-Baker and M. Baker, *The Life and Circumstances of James Brydges, 1st Duke of Chandos*, London, 1949, 83–92. Thornhill, when asked to assess their recent ruinous restoration, thought Chandos had been "grossly abused" by Christopher Cock, the restorer. He demurred from testifying in the law suit brought by Chandos, probably because he had not seen the cartoons before they were restored.

120. Chandos proposed that if Davenant could find a buyer he could have them for £100 less than they cost, and he sug-

remarked upon in passing when at Kirby Hall (the one house having been demolished and the other built circa 1747), there is no compelling reason to doubt their provenance. Confirmation of their authenticity, however, does not depend upon this inconclusive trail of ownership and can be established on other bases.

Vertue's emphasis of Thornhill's fidelity to Raphael raises the question of whether Thornhill's "hand" is at all evident, whether Thornhill's brush can be recognized (as distinct, for example, from that of Jervas), when truthful replication demands suppressing the copyist's personal style. Compounding the problem is that despite Thornhill's intention to preserve Raphael's ideas in a more enduring form, his own copies eventually fell into disrepair and under the hands of restorers.[121] In their favor is that the paintings do answer Vertue's description in their dimensions and full-strength oil finish. Further support for the traditional ascription is provided by some verifiable preliminary drawings by Thornhill. Many were listed in the sale of his collection of prints, drawings, and casts in 1734/5, as in the following six lots:[122]

(1) A Large portofolio with several off Tracts upon Oyl'd Paper from the Cartoons
(15) A portfolio of Heads, Arms, &c. of the Cartoons
(18) A large Portfolio of off Tracts from the Cartoons
(19) Ditto with draughts for the lesser Cartoons
(20) Ditto
(21) Ditto

Today two albums of Thornhill drawings are known whose contents probably come from those portfolios. One, an oblong album (12 1/2 by 15 inches) with about two hundred large drawings can be identified with a set described in 1889 as a "torn bundle of old tracings which came into my possession some years ago. . . . They number over two hundred, and are fairly well preserved. On one of these is written 'Legg of St. Andrew J. T. 1729.'"[123] These same drawings resurfaced in 1936, when they were purchased by the dean of Saint Paul's Cathedral. By this time the sheets were no longer bundled, having been mounted in an album incorrectly identified as sketches primarily for the eight scenes of the life of Saint Paul that Thornhill designed for the cupola.[124] The drawings are, in fact, tracings of various heads, hands, and limbs and of architectural details that Thornhill made directly from Raphael's originals (figs. 27, 28, 30, 32, 59, 63, 65, 66, 68).[125] The rendering is in brush and brown ink over black chalk; some of the drawings are in simple outline, others vigorously

gested on 30 March 1724 that Robert Walpole might take the four cartoons for £1200.

121. In 1968, thickly encrusted dirt and varnish were removed and the canvases were relined anew, the lining of some forty years earlier having worked loose. *The Miraculous Draught of Fishes* in particular shows definite signs of restoration.

122. Thornhill Sale B, 26 February, Portfolio F.

123. *Notes & Queries*, series 7, VII, 20 April 1889, 306 (signed "Rb. Rb. Lawton").

124. My thanks to Brian Tuppen for calling these drawings to my attention. Most likely purchased from a dealer, the album is (incorrectly) identified by a printed label as an "Album of Sketches by Sir James Thornhill, many of them of the figures he painted in the Eight Scenes in the Life of Saint Paul in the cupola. Others were used by him in the ceilings at Windsor Castle, Hampton Court Palace, Greenwich Palace and elsewhere. One is initialed and dated 1729."

125. For Walpole's reference to these studies by Thornhill, see p. 64.

FIGS. 27, 28, 30, 32 James Thornhill (after Raphael), *The Lame Man Healed*, ca.1729, brush and brown ink, from an album of tracings, 10 x 14 in., Saint Paul's Cathedral, London

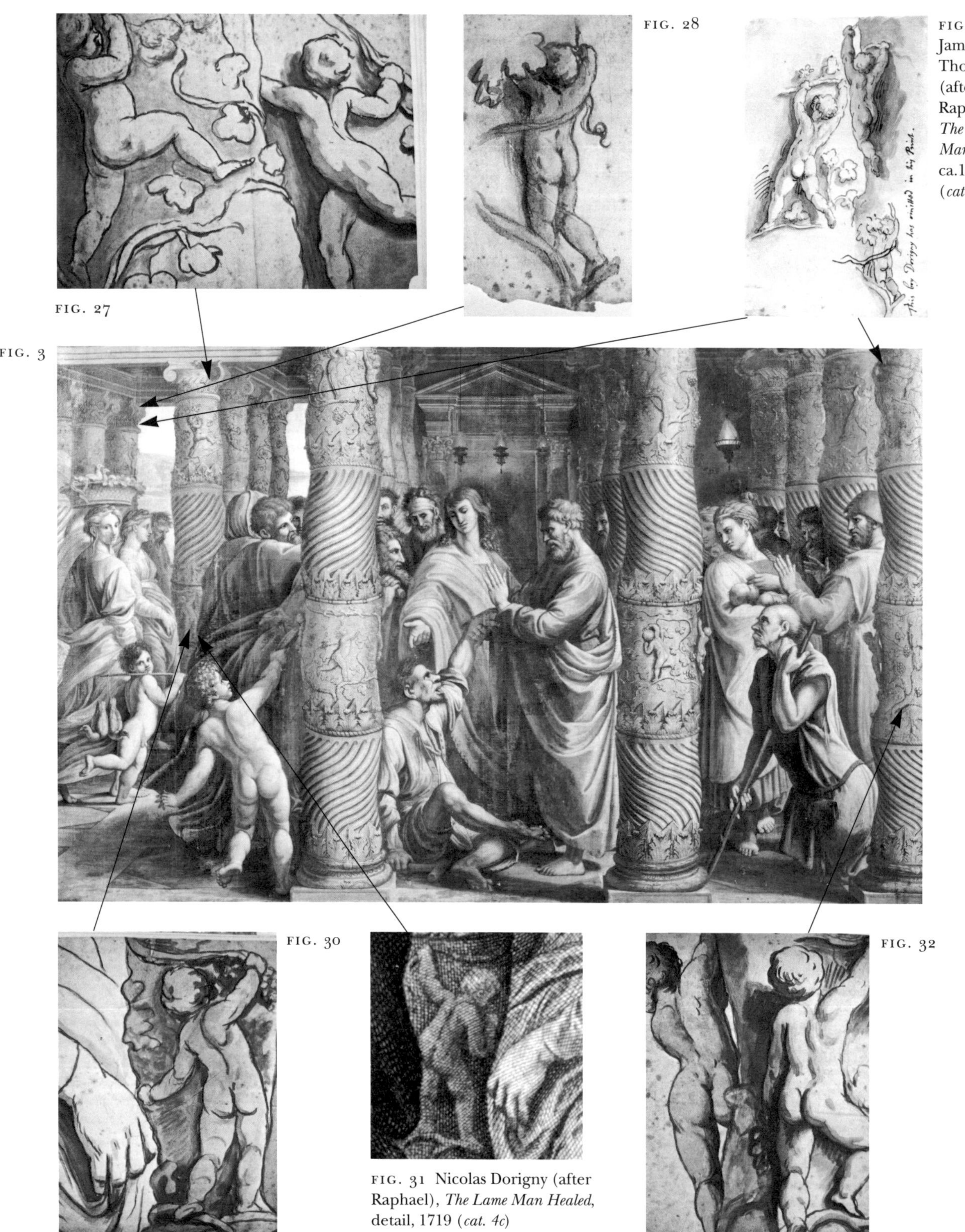

FIG. 27

FIG. 28

FIG. 29 James Thornhill (after Raphael), *The Lame Man Healed*, ca.1729–31 (*cat. 31*)

FIG. 3

FIG. 30

FIG. 31 Nicolas Dorigny (after Raphael), *The Lame Man Healed*, detail, 1719 (*cat. 4c*)

FIG. 32

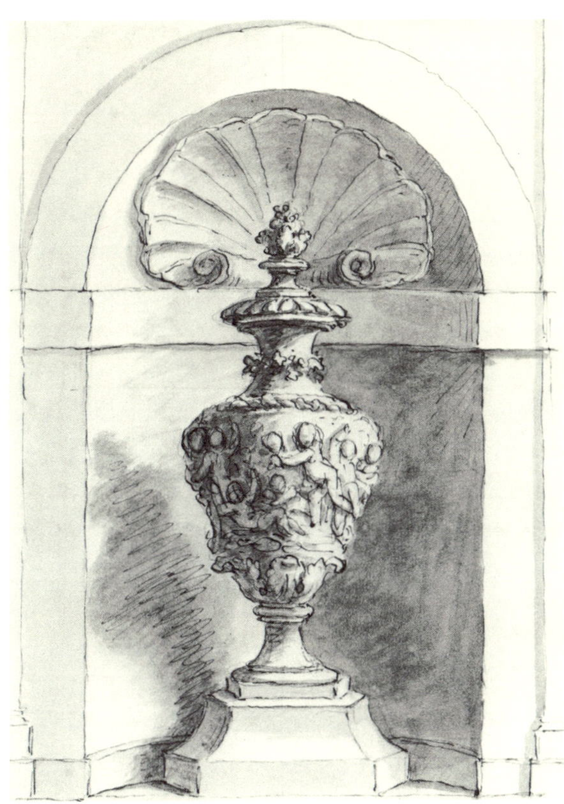

FIG. 33 James Thornhill, *A Niche for Mr. Portman's House at Sherborne*, detail (*cat. 40*)

modeled with wash. This is in perfect accord with Vertue's description of "several studies of the heads hands feets. separately &c. from these originals on paper drawn out lines some shaded. some not are surely the truest & justest demonstration of Raphaels merit, excellent talent of any that ever was."[126]

The second album contains 162 small drawings, each measuring about 4½ by 6¾ inches, randomly mounted three or four per page (figs. 29, 37–44, 60, 62).[127] Here Thornhill has drawn with a pen rather than a brush. Compared with the lively style of the large drawings, these smaller ones are somewhat timid and mechanical. This may be partly because they are in a different medium, but more likely because they are drawings of drawings, scaled-down reductions of the various heads and limbs found in the larger album.

It is in tracings of certain details–details that are now barely decipherable in Raphael's original Cartoons–that Thornhill's authorship of the Columbia paintings can be confirmed. At times the tracings clarify murky passages in the originals (fig. 28), and this heightened definition of form has in turn been transferred to the paintings, as for example in the treatment of John's sandaled foot in *Christ's Charge to Peter* (fig. 2). Additionally, in both the drawings and the paintings there is evidence of Thornhill's efforts to restore losses and to correct poor restorations. Thornhill seems to have been especially interested in the ornamental details of the twisted columns in *The Lame Man Healed* (fig. 3); he made many tracings of the small nude boys who frolic among the grapevines (figs. 27–30, 32), and later exploited the motif decoratively (fig. 33). On a small sketch of one such figure Thornhill noted, "this boy Dorigny omitted from his engraving" (fig. 29), and a comparison between figs. 30 and 31 shows Dorigny was inattentive in the rendering of other details. While the figure he singled out is scarcely visible in the Cartoon, it is included in the Columbia copy. Furthermore, the distinctive shorthand Thornhill used to render the ambling foliage on the columns (e.g., fig. 27) is stylistically the same in both the painting and the drawings.

126. Vertue III, 39 (August 1729). W. R. Osmun claims that Vertue took exception to Thornhill's studies of details which he felt did not do justice to Raphael. Yet, because of Vertue's characteristically bizarre punctuation, Osmun misread "some not" (in the text quoted) as referring to "the truest & justest . . . etc.," whereas the phrase actually refers to "drawn outlines some shaded. some not" which is an accurate description of how the drawings are rendered ("A Study of the Works of Sir James Thornhill," Ph.D. diss., University of London, 1950, 120).

127. Some of the drawings are mounted upside down, and in one instance what appears to be a leg is actually a shoulder.

IV. RAPHAEL'S CARTOONS: IN THEORY AND PRACTICE

JONATHAN RICHARDSON: PROMOTING RAPHAEL IN ENGLAND

RAPHAEL HAD A PROFOUND influence on the theory and practice of art in the eighteenth century. From the time of Vasari's *Lives* (1568), his work was proclaimed in theoretical treatises on painting as the benchmark of excellence. More than from any other artist, it was his repertoire of compositions, postures, and expressions that painters borrowed and quoted.[128]

Both as an idea and as a model Raphael had a far longer lineage in France than in England.[129] The French image of Raphael is rooted first of all in Vasari and in the descriptions by later Italian theorists–Ludovico Dolce, Frederico Zuccaro, Giovanni Paolo Lomazzo, and Giovan Pietro Bellori. Subsequently, French painters and amateurs–Fréart de Chambray, André Félibien, Alphonse Du Fresnoy, and Roger de Piles–promoted him as the supreme exemplar of proper design, invention, and expression. The French School had been honed on High Renaissance models since the early seventeenth century, and by the 1660s the French Academy had culled from those models the classical precepts that formed the basis of its programmatic instruction. It was primarily via Poussin that Renaissance classicism shaped French art. His paintings were frequently the focal subject of the Academy's *Conférences* and were so revered as instructive examples that he earned the sobriquet the "French Raphael."

England lagged more than a hundred years behind her continental neighbor in creating a distinctly national school. The promising encouragement given to the arts and to native English talent by the patronage of Charles I was unfortunately short-lived, and the hope of a cultural florescence was deferred by years of civil war. When the monarchy was restored in 1660, England begin a cultural recovery and, however grudgingly, looked to France for guidance. The burgeoning interest in improving the arts created a profitable market in England for translations of French treatises, and in the first decade of the eighteenth century London booksellers were offering the *Conference of Monsieur Le Brun Upon Expression* (1701), Félibien's *Tent of Darius Explain'd* (1703), De Piles's *Art of Painting* (1708), and various derivative works. Nevertheless, there was scant acknowledgment of this French literary filter, for when it came to choosing a model of artistic taste English artists looked directly to *Rafaello d'Urbino.*

Although the Tapestry Cartoons had been installed at Hampton Court in 1699, they remained largely unsung through the next decade–apart from an effusive poetic tribute that Richard Blackmore appended in 1703 to his Miltonesque "Hymn to the Light of the World."[130]

128. The language of such artistic activity has been updated—though the activity substantially is unaltered—to consider the various strategies painters have employed in "turning the tradition" of Raphael. This kinetic three-dimensional description is used by N. Bryson in *Tradition and Desire: From David to Delacroix,* New York, 1990, xvii–xviii.

129. For a discussion of "The Creation of a French Raphael," see Rosenberg 1995, 22–30.

130. *A Hymn to the Light of the World. With a short description of the Cartons of Raphael Urbin, in the Gallery at Hampton-court,* London, 1703. Alas, his couplets bolstered neither Raphael's cause nor the cause of religious poetry, both of which he zealously championed. He later praised Raphael in an essay "The Parallel between Poetry and Painting," published in the *Lay Monastery,* 1714. See A. Rosenberg, *Sir Richard Blackmore: A Poet and Physician of the Augustan Age,* Lincoln, NB, 1953, 81–83.

It was only in 1711, in an essay by Richard Steele, that the Hampton Court Cartoons and their maker emerged as catalysts for ideas. Steele eloquently lauded both Raphael's paintings and his person on aesthetic, moral, and religious grounds and called for public support of Nicolas Dorigny's proposal to engrave the Cartoons.[131]

In the second decade of the century, in his first published treatise, *The Theory of Painting* (1715), Jonathan Richardson time and again summoned the Cartoons as supreme examples of invention, expression, composition, and (with some restraint in praise) of coloring. His accommodating judgments and succinct characterizations of Raphael made a lasting impression on his audience: his praise of licentious indulgence (because of the inauthentic but magnificent spiral columns) in the *Healing of the Lame Man* (fig. 3) and his description of Elymas as "blind from head to foot" (fig. 5) are two of his many observations that were repeated by those who subsequently wrote on the Cartoons.[132]

Richardson gave a distinctly British spin to the theory of painting. His *Two Discourses* (1719) are among the most remarkable and programmatic texts on connoisseurship in the entire literature of art.[133] In these essays—"The Art of Criticism" (concerned with how to judge paintings) and "The Science of a Connoisseur" (why that would be a worthwhile pursuit)—Richardson took a scientific approach. He presented his ideas in the language of empirical philosophy, thereby engaging his audience by using the familiar vocabulary of Shaftesbury and Locke. But his zealous attempt to render ideas visible through the medium of language produced some rather novel prose; and, as Walpole noted,[134] his pragmatic judgments of good common sense often were marred by their labored and quaint expression. His idiosyncratic style gave sporting ammunition to his critics. Some French writers, shocked by his critical independence, regarded his confident censure of canonical works as aesthetic heresy.[135] Yet Richardson's was still an English voice to be reckoned with.

Richardson promoted Raphael's merits in all of his theoretical essays on painting and connoisseurship, but he did so at greatest length in his guide to the works of art in Italy, *An Account of Some of the Statues, Bas-Reliefs, Drawings, and Pictures in Italy, &c., with Remarks* (1722). Apparently the impulse to publish the *Account* stemmed from the series of methodically descriptive letters that his son Jonathan Richardson Jr. wrote for his father's pleasure during his travel abroad in 1720–21. The letters were just a starting point, however, since Richardson Sr. substantially expanded upon his son's observations. The book was ostensibly a travel guide, but the first edition typically served the armchair connoisseur, for whom Richardson aimed to be a tutor rather than a tour guide.[136] Whereas he believed that most

131. See pp. 28–29.

132. The author of the "Description of the Cartoons of Raphael Urbin" (see pp. 3–16) cites Richardson as the authority who has carefully studied the Cartoons and often repeats observations made in the *Theory of Painting*.

133. Gibson-Wood 1984, 38. This article offers an acute reassessment of Richardson's contribution.

134. Walpole IV, 17.

135. In the preface to his translation from the Italian of Ludovico Dolce's *Dialogue on Painting*, Nicolas Vleughels challenged Richardson's judgments on Raphael (Hercenberg, *Nicolas Vleughels*, 189). But in Richardson's introduction to the *Account*, he already anticipated that "The Abatements we have made from the Common, receiv'd Opinion with relation to Some Celebrated Works may be Censur'd. We Expect it."

136. It was only with the second edition, published in 1754, that Richardson's book became the de rigueur companion for the grand tour. For this edition the title was subtly altered to appear more comprehensive: *An Account of the Statues, Bas-Reliefs, Drawings, and Pictures in Italy, France, &c., with Remarks.*

Italian writers on art tended to injudicious declamations (rather than description) and were apt to give encomiums to trifles,[137] the travel book format gave him the perfect vehicle for applying the rules he had outlined in his essays to specific pictures and statues.

THE HAMPTON COURT CARTOONS VERSUS THE VATICAN STANZE FRESCOES

The centerpiece of Richardson's *Account* is an extremely detailed appraisal of Raphael's frescoes in the Vatican Stanze that runs to 70 of the book's 350 pages. Although he paid homage to the frescoes' beauties, Richardson apparently felt no qualms about veering from received opinion on these celebrated works, and likewise noted their defects, their "blackish and disagreeable" condition,[138] and their dark situation, in gloomy, unpopulated rooms "forsaken by painters, lovers, and even by the Pope himself."[139] These criticisms, however, were but a prelude to his argument for the nobler and more accomplished Raphael that could be seen at Hampton Court. In his earlier essays Richardson had frequently used drawings in his own collection when discussing the works at hand. In the *Account* he advanced public rather than private treasures when he cited the Cartoons as the most masterly examples of Raphael's art:

> One may have an Idea of the Merit of the Pictures done by Raffaele himself, by comparing them with those of Him at *Hampton-Court*: Here is that Greatness of Style, those Noble Attitudes; Airs of Heads, and even the like Pencil and Coloring; Only These are not so Gay, and Pleasing; which is Partly Owing to the Coloring it self, and Partly to Circumstances I have been remarking; the want of Harmony, the Disadvantageous Positions, the Darkness, and not a Little to the *Gothic* Old-fashion'd Place, and That Heighten'd by its being Uninhabited, and Unfrequented, which together with the Rest spreads a sort of Melancholy Air throughout, Especially in the Rooms painted by Raffaele himself, which (as I said) want Light extremely.[140]

By the end of his discussion Richardson declared an open competition by noting that the Vatican apartments "have the Greatest Collection of the Works of the Greatest Painter in the World; but withal that they are not Altogether what one would naturally expect from the great Fame they have, and the Name they are Adorn'd with. *Raffaele* is seen Here indeed, but not So as to give a Just Idea of his Merit." Richardson goes on to express doubt that the full extent of Raphael's genius can be glimpsed in any single painting, palace, or collection, but informs his reader that one can come close, for "there is a Palace where one may receive a Higher, a Juster, and a more Complete Idea of him than Here, or any where Else, and that

137. Richardson 1722, 157.

138. Their blackened condition was probably worsened by the aged Carlo Maratta, who, when entrusted with the restoration of Raphael's frescoes by Clement XI, washed them down with wine (L. von Pastor, *The History of the Popes*, XXXIII, London, 1957, 514).

139. Richardson 1722, 194.

140. Ibid., 198. A century later G. F. Waagen criticized Wren's gallery for the poor visibility of the Cartoons: "In a long, lofty, but narrow apartment, wainscoted with brown oak, and scantily lighted by twelve low, narrow windows, the cartoons are hung in such a manner, that the lower edge of them, about eleven feet from the ground, is only about a foot lower than the top of the windows, by which means they only receive from below a very subdued light. This light is at least diffused pretty equally over the five which hang on the long side opposite to the windows; but part of the two others, which hang on the two ends is wholly concealed from the eyes of the friends of art by a dark shadow. A second row of windows, at a greater height, with corresponding intervals, is designedly walled up. Under these circumstances, no notion can be formed of the effect which these miracles of art would produce, if they were placed in a full side light falling from above" (*Works of Art and Artists in England*, London, 1838, 2:88–89).

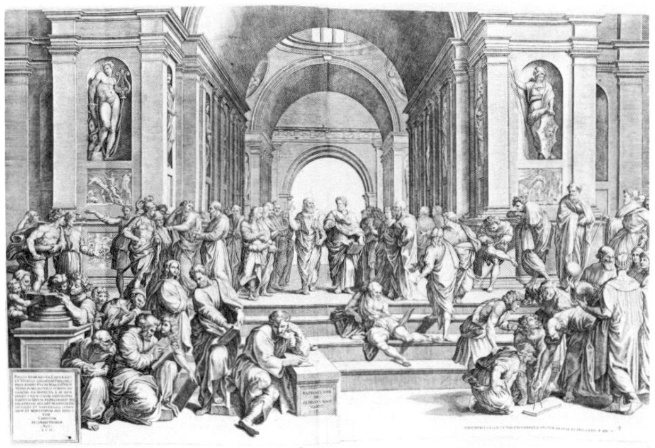

FIG. 34 Giorgio Ghisi (after Raphael), *School of Athens*, 1550 (*cat. 7*)

is *Hampton-Court.*"[141] By way of methodical, point by point comparison of such factors as dignity of subject matter, thoughts conveyed, portable versus fixed paintings, and specifics of rendering, coloring, drawing, and composition, Richardson concluded that Raphael's works at Hampton Court outshone their counterparts at the Vatican, for the Cartoons achieved "Such Perfection as what is Humane is capable of."[142]

Richardson's announcement that "Hampton-Court is the great School of Rafaelle!" was more than an acknowledgment of a national treasure. His subsequent remarks in the *Theory of Painting* were in the nature of a religious supplication calling for the exemption of such divine creations from the forces of decay:

> . . . and God be praised that we have so near us such an invaluable Blessing. May the Cartons continue in That Place, and always to be seen; Unhurt, and Undecay'd, so long as the Nature of the Materials of which they are compos'd will possibly allow. May even a Miracle be wrought in their favor, as Themselves are some of the greatest Instances of the Divine Power which endured a Mortal Man with Abilities to perform such Stupendous Works of Art.[143]

To score points in this arena was less an attempt to upstage Rome than an effort to bolster England's position in relation to France. The Stanze served as the main training ground for students at the French Academy in Rome. In 1670 a directive from Paris had made it mandatory that pensioners copy the Vatican frescoes in full size.[144] While this gave French academicians a firm grounding in Raphael, England could now boast a superior training ground, and on home turf at that.

Nor was Richardson's assessment of Raphael an exercise in abstract theorizing on the principles of artistic excellence. Rather, it was closely tied to his interest in the practical application of such ideas, if not in actual artistic practice in England at the time, then at least toward implementing a rational course of study for English artists. Thus the appearance of Richardson's *Account* in 1722–although couched in the format of a travel guide–dovetailed with a more widespread interest in forming an officially sanctioned academy and with issues of artistic patronage.

141. Richardson 1722, 250–51.

142. Ibid., 255.

143. Richardson (1715) 1725, 115–16.

144. Rosenberg 1979, 69–70.

TOWARD AN ENGLISH ACADEMY

The first sustained evidence of artists assembling with a sense of professional urgency was in 1711, with the opening of an academy in Great Queen Street.[145] While it was a private institution, and not the "royal academy" that some of its members had pressed for as early as 1698, it was nonetheless a foundation stone for the official Royal Academy that would receive its charter from the Crown in 1768. Thornhill was one of its twelve elected directors and with some sixty fellow artists and supporters was involved in setting up the once grand but now decayed mansion that served as its quarters.[146] The early years of the academy, however, were plagued with constant rivalries, which considerably hindered the efforts of English painters to improve their training and to augment their purses, patronage, and artistic reputations.[147] Thornhill repeatedly jockeyed to secure the management of the academy from its governor, the portrait painter Godfrey Kneller; and after years of sparring, he finally prevailed in 1716, but only after his older rival had resigned.[148]

While Kneller did not envision the academy as a national institution[149] (his notion of its function was apparently limited to his parochial interest as a portraitist), several elected directors–Thornhill among them–did actively seek the Crown's support. In addition, in 1714 Thornhill presented Lord Halifax, first lord treasurer, with architectural plans for housing an academy in apartments near the King's Mews, with the hope of receiving official sponsorship.[150] Richardson also argued the academy's cause in 1719 in a lengthy passage in "The Science of a Connoisseur." Though he too was a portraitist, Richardson conceived a course of broad-ranging study using examples of modern drawings and ancient statuary (be they originals or copies) for instruction.[151] As in all of Richardson's essays, Raphael loomed large as the preeminent model for imitation. His conception of an academy stretched beyond a mere technical training ground and aimed at polishing English sensibility. To this end, the example of the sublime Raphael could best hurry English gentlemen along in the civilizing

145. For the most comprehensive account of the history of various art academies and clubs in London prior to the founding of the Royal Academy, and of Vertue as a chronicler of the arts, see I. Bignamini, "George Vertue, Art Historian, and Art Institutions in London 1689–1768," *Walpole Society*, LIV, 1991, 1–148.

146. Great Queen Street had been a very fashionable locale in the seventeenth century but subsequently became a quarter for artists (Whitley, 1:7–8).

147. Factional rivalries were the norm; earlier in his career, Thornhill had beaten out Chéron, Laguerre, Pellegrini, and Ricci for prized commissions, but by 1722, when William Kent secured a coveted painting commission at Kensington Palace, significant changes in the artistic pecking order were already apparent. Although several of Thornhill's rivals had been silenced, or rather buried—Laguerre had died in 1721, Kneller in 1723, and Chéron in 1725—the new center of activity focused on Lord Burlington and his protégé William Kent.

148. As might be expected, Thornhill in turn was deposed by another faction, led by Louis Chéron and John Vanderbank, who formed an academy at a new location in St. Martin's Lane in 1720. Thornhill set up a school at his own house in Covent Garden, but with a diminished following it did not last long. The St. Martin's Lane Academy—despite the setback it suffered when the treasurer embezzled subscriptions—went into a successful second phase in 1735, under the guidance of Thornhill's son-in-law, William Hogarth (Whitley, 1:26–27).

Thornhill must have been deeply irritated that Raphael's famous Latin epitaph, "Raphael, timuit quo sospite, vinci /Rerum magna parens, & moriente, mori," was translated by Alexander Pope and then applied to Kneller, "Living, great Nature fear'd he might outvie/Her works; and dying, fears herself may die" ("Epitaph. on Sir Godfrey Kneller, In Westminster–Abbey 1723"). See Whitley, 1:54.

149. Ibid., 62–63.

150. Thornhill's plan failed to interest Halifax (ibid., 1:14).

151. Richardson 1773, 278.

process. No one was better able to mentor that progress than Richardson, for, as Walpole remarked, no man dived deeper than he into the inexhaustible stores of Raphael.[152]

Despite the contentious atmosphere at the academy, the 1710s was a decade of lively English engagement in the arts. A written narrative of those strides began in 1712, in the second year of the Great Queen Street Academy, when George Vertue—a young engraver still waiting on his reputation—began compiling notes on London's artistic scene. Not surprisingly, Raphael's name is steadily laced through some fifty years of his copious judgments and jottings.[153]

PUBLISHERS AND THE BOOK TRADE: PROMOTING RAPHAEL IN ENGLAND

In the story of this seemingly altruistic celebration of Raphael, both in theoretical treatises and more informally among artists focused on practical modes of instruction, a more commercial factor comes into play. The commercial book and print trade was a major agent for disseminating ideas and for making reputations, and consequently publishers and print sellers deserve the credit for initiating some of the century's most influential publications. Even if the driving impulse was marketability rather than content, much of the progress in England in the art of engraving was a direct result of publisher's commissions.[154] It even seems likely that the idea for Richardson's *Account* was initiated by James Knapton, his publisher. Knapton may well have hoped that Richardson's unusual "connoisseur's guide" would follow the success of William Dampier's *Voyages and Descriptions* (1703).[155] Richardson's curiously defensive preface (where he preempts criticism in a lengthy recitation of anticipated complaints)[156] suggests that he may have been prodded to publish, and clearly he was far more interested in how his ideas would be received than in monetary gain; relinquishing the standard premium, Richardson made the unusual arrangement for his publisher to give away handsomely bound copies of his book to a number of gentlemen whose opinions he respected.[157]

Thornhill was also involved in several publishing projects, and these directly related to his studies of the Raphael Cartoons. One involved drawings showing Raphael's paintings in their present as well as their earlier state (revised and etched shortly before he died in 1734 but never published). Another scheme of broader interest—also left unfinished—was a

152. But adding "One wonders that he could comment on their works so well, and imitate them so little" (Walpole IV, 16).

153. See n. 21.

154. Colen Campbell's *Vitruvius Britannicus* was one such undertaking (see E. Harris, "'Vitruvius Britannicus' before Colen Campbell," *Burlington Magazine*, MXXVIII, May 1986, 340–46), as was Hogarth's early narrative series Hudibras, and the series of prints on The Life of Charles I, done in imitation of the Marie de' Medici cycle at the Luxembourg Palace (Vertue IV, 190–91).

155. James Knapton was a leading member in the Wholesaling Conger, the small group of copyright-owning booksellers that wielded formidable control in the period following the 1710 Copyright Act. Knapton took on large, costly editions that often took years to see the shelves, and the copyright he owned on Dampier's *Voyages* was the lifeblood of the family business (*Dictionary of Literary Biography: The British Literary Book Trade, 1700–1820*, 1995, 154: 170–75).

156. Richardson knew he would be chided by his detractors for writing about Italy's artistic treasures, having never made the journey or seen what he described.

157. This arrangement rankled Vertue; he had numerous complaints about the book, and he equated distributing free copies in this manner with the vile practice of hawkers of religious tracts (Vertue MSS., f. 90r and Gibson-Wood 1982, 275).

handbook for students of painting and sculpture that featured engravings of heads, hands, feet, and other details from the Cartoons.[158] These projects possibly were conceived in the aftermath of the publication of Richardson's guidebook to Italy in 1722, in which Raphael had played such a central role.

Also in 1722 (and probably not by coincidence), a collection of prints related to the Cartoons was published. Eight French engravers were engaged to produce the plates that were based on Dorigny's drawings of ninety heads from the Cartoons.[159] There was no text apart from its discursive title page:

> Recueil de XC Têtes Tirées des Sept Cartons des Actes Des Apôtres Peints Par Raph. 'Urbin, qui se conservent dans Le Palais d'Hampton-Court, dessinées par le Chevr. Nic. Dorigny, et gravées par les meilleurs graveurs, mis en lumière à Londres l'an 1722 et dedié a Son altesse Royale Madame La Princesse de Galles par sa tres humble tres obeissite et tres respectueuse Serv.te Marie Maugis.

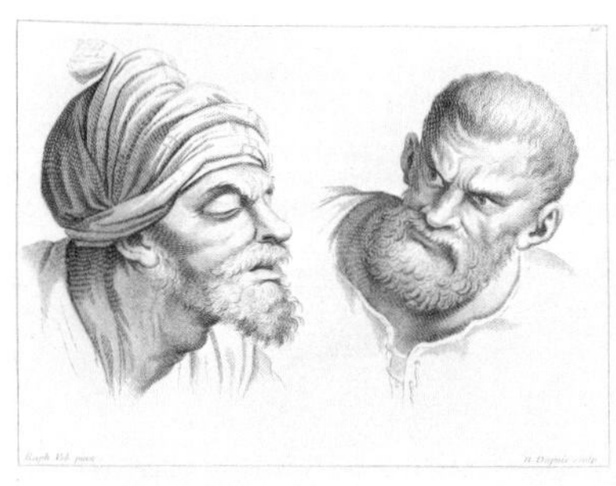

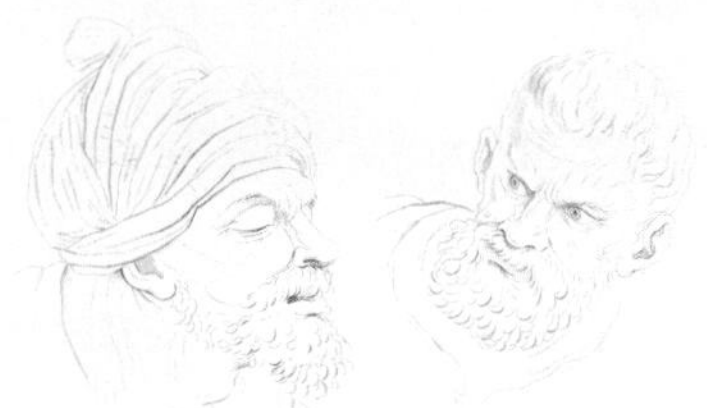

FIG. 35 "Arrogance Dejected" and "Astonishment and Doubt," plate 26 in *School of Raphael*, London, 1759 (*cat. 23*)

These prints, apparently intended for the export market, seem to have had very limited circulation. Their distribution may have been stalled by the economic problems that plagued both sides of the Channel in the early 1720s, with the subsequent disruption of the book and print trade between England and France.[160]

In 1759 the *Recueil* was completely repackaged and expanded into a commercially viable edition titled *The School of Raphael* under the imprint of John Boydell.[161] It was enlarged to 102 copper plates and 14 sheets of letter press; the addition of engraved outlines of the heads expanded the original number of 45 plates (two heads per plate) to 90 (fig. 35); and 12 plates of proportion, anatomy, body parts, and celebrated antique statues were also added. It appears that some few remnants of Thornhill's unrealized plan for a drawing manual made their way into some of these plates unheralded: fourteen of the engraved details of arms, legs, hands, and feet (fig. 36)[162] perfectly match Thornhill's small sketches in the album in the Victoria and Albert Museum (figs. 37–44).

158. Vertue III, 70.

159. The number of heads by each is as follows: N. Beauvais (10); B. Lépicié (2); N.-G. Dupuis (12); G. Duchange (8); L. Desplaces (8); N. Pigné (40); N. H. Tardieu (2); H. S. Thomassin (8). All the engravers, except for Duchange, were known to have resided in England at least for a time, but only two of the plates (by Pigné) are specifically inscribed "sculp. Lond."

160. G. Barber, *Studies in the Booktrade of the European Enlightenment*, London, 1994, 232. Copies of the *Recueil* are rare. I have only found two: one in London in the Library of the Royal Academy; another (incomplete copy) in Paris at the Bibliothèque Nationale, which Alisa Luxemberg kindly located.

161. An intermediary issue of the *Recueil* under Boydell's imprint can be dated somewhere between 1751/52 and 1754, the terminus ante quem being the date he opened a shop in Cheapside and the terminus post quem when a decision was taken to expand the publication more fully. In this issue, an English translation was added to the original French title page, and the publication included descriptions of the seven Cartoons and an index identifying each of the 90 heads with a specific "Passion."

162. Some of the other details in these plates are not even from the Cartoons, but were taken from some other source.

The form of the book is an assemblage of the sort that typically was initiated by a publisher in possession of a copperplate stock,[163] rather than by an individual author, with supplementary prints derived from earlier antiquarian and scientific publications.[164] This popular spin-off from the Cartoons was not simply a set of engravings for the print collector but a book designed to appeal to amateurs, artists, and the general public. An advertisement for the book gives an account of the original plates and of the genesis of the publication:

> The celebrated Sir Nicholas Dorigny having caused the principal Heads in the Cartons to be engraved, by several eminent French Engravers, from his own Drawings, and under his immediate Inspection, the Plates were, some Years ago, purchased in France by a very ingenious Gentleman; and being brought to England, became some Time afterwards the Property of the Editor.
>
> In the Year 1754, it was thought, that by adding a Number of Plates, describing the Rudiments of Design, the Anatomy of the Human Body, and Several of the best Antique Statues, a most useful and elegant Drawing Book might be made, in order to give young Students a true Taste of Design, and an early Acquaintance with the great Ideas of Raphael: accordingly the Book came out, under the Title of *The School of Raphael*; to which was prefixed An Essay on the Art of Design; in which, the Rules for attaining so polite and useful an Accomplishment were laid down according to the most approved methods; and also the following Description of the Cartons, referring to the Several Heads in that Collection, and explaining their Characters, and the particular Figures to which they belong.[165]

The Description of the Cartoons is reprinted on pp. 3–16 above. Who wrote the text remains uncertain. The title page identified the author as Benjamin Ralph, who now proves to be a shadowy figure.[166] The frequency of pseudonymous publications in this era, however,

163. Although *The School of Raphael* was republished with a new title page in 1782 and in 1825, the book actually went through innumerable issues that were not proper editions. Rather, the new issues were composed largely of sheets derived from the original setting but often with a new title page and some new additions. The book appeared in many such "scrap" or "harlequin" editions and in the early nineteenth century was sometimes bound with Reynolds's *Discourses*. Its various sheets often were scrambled and at times interleaved with an unlikely assortment of landscape prints. See Barber, *Studies in the Booktrade*, 110 and n. 11.

The catalogue of Boydell's stock in 1803 (*An alphabetical Catalogue of Plates, engraved by the most esteemed artists, after the finest pictures and drawings of the Italian, Flemish, German, French, English, and other schools which compose the stock of John and Josiah Boydell, Engravers and Printsellers, preceded by an account of various works, sets of prints, galleries etc., forming part of the same stock*, London, 1803) and the catalogue of his stock when sold in 1818 (*A Catalogue of more than five thousand copper plates . . . etc. comprising the entire stock of Messrs. John and Josiah Boydell, deceased June 1–June 6 1818*) list not only the plates and bound copies of *The School of Raphael* but folios of various unbound sections.

164. Three prints of classical sculpture in *The School of Raphael* (Belvedere Torso, Apollo Belvedere, Farnese Hercules) are re-engravings of plates in Domenico de Rossi's canonical corpus *Raccolte di Statue Antiche e Moderne* (Rome, 1704). Four anatomical illustrations derive from Bernhard Siegried Albinus's *Tabulae Scheleti et Muscolorum Corporis Humani*.

165. The advertisement appeared in the front of B. Ralph, *A Description of The Cartoons of Raphael Urbin, in The Queen's Palace*, London, 1764, a book that reprinted sections of *The School of Raphael*. The accuracy of this account is not at all certain since the plates may well have been identified as coming from France to give them extra cachet. This was a period when the traffic was all in one direction, when thousands of pounds of foreign engravings were imported yearly and when no English engravings were exported. See T. Balston, "John Boydell, Publisher," *Signature*, no. 8, n.s., 1949, 3–22. If Dorigny owned the plates it seems unlikely that he would have taken them with him when he finally returned to Paris on 9 April 1724 (date from Vertue III, 19), since much of his work was sold at auction before he left London (see n. 51).

166. If Reynolds had this popular publication in mind when he complained of writers fond of describing the expression of the mixed passions with great exactness (precisely what this publication attempts), his identification of such writers on art as "not being of the profession" implies its author is clearly not a painter (Reynolds, 78). If such is the case, then it seems unlikely that the author is the landscape painter by that name who is known to have exhibited occassionally at the Society of Artists in the 1760s and '70s, as suggested by S. Dickey ("The Passions and Raphael's Cartoons in Eighteenth-Century British Art," *Marsyas*, XXII, 1986, 33–46). In

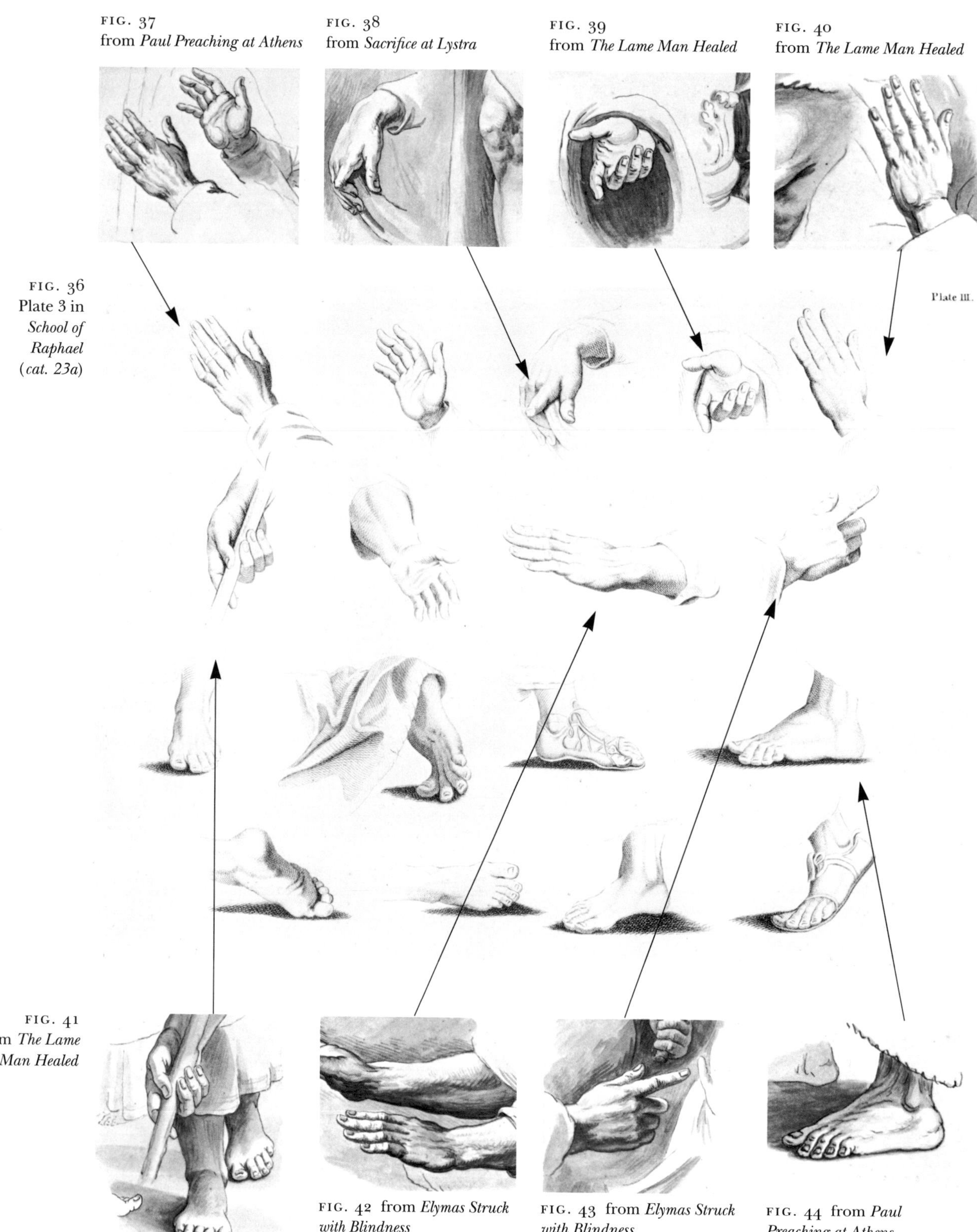

FIG. 37 from *Paul Preaching at Athens*

FIG. 38 from *Sacrifice at Lystra*

FIG. 39 from *The Lame Man Healed*

FIG. 40 from *The Lame Man Healed*

FIG. 36 Plate 3 in *School of Raphael* (*cat. 23a*)

FIG. 41 from *The Lame Man Healed*

FIG. 42 from *Elymas Struck with Blindness*

FIG. 43 from *Elymas Struck with Blindness*

FIG. 44 from *Paul Preaching at Athens*

FIGS. 37–44 James Thornhill (after Raphael), ca. 1729–31 (*cat. 31*)

suggests that Benjamin Ralph may indeed be a fictional name. In view of the content and tone of some of the introductory remarks to *The School of Raphael*, it would appear to have been authored by someone in Hogarth's inner circle. Viable candidates would be James Ralph (1705?–1762),[167] Hogarth's friend and neighbor in Chiswick and an outspoken journalist who wrote on painting and architectural subjects for the *Weekly Register*, and Benjamin Wilson,[168] a fellow artist with Hogarth at the St. Martin's Lane Academy who helped Hogarth formulate his ideas for the *Analysis of Beauty*.

Authorship aside, the idea for this popular book most likely came from the commercially savvy John Boydell. His study of the rudiments of drawing at the St. Martin's Lane Academy in the 1740s apprised him of a ready market for an instructional guide that was more comprehensive than those available. In 1751 Boydell took a membership in the Stationer's Company and established a successful shop at the corner of Queen Street and Cheapside, where, specializing in the sale of reproductive prints, he deftly assembled plates into folios.[169] *The School of Raphael* which presents the Cartoons as a significant instrument of academic instruction in England (Richardson redux in a somewhat more tangible form)[170] was a direct outgrowth of the mushrooming academies in London early in the century.

"THE SCHOOL OF RAPHAEL" AND MID-CENTURY ACADEMY POLITICS

The School of Raphael is both an artist's manual and a proclamation. On the one hand the illustrations and text describe a course of study; on the other they demonstrate how closely allied aesthetic issues were to nationalistic and religious concerns. The book's long-term success (it remained in print through 1825) is perhaps best seen in the context of artistic politics of the late 1750s, for the ideas it expresses summarize the concerns of that loose community of artists who gathered in various drawing academies and coffeehouses in London—a somewhat disunited, if not to say disgruntled, body. Although the leading portraitists prospered, other artists had no venue for exhibiting their work and no assurance of public or official support. Numerous meetings were held at the St. Martin's Lane Academy[171] in hope of establishing an official academy that would improve the lot of English artists by making them less dependent upon picture dealers for their livelihood. Hogarth played a central role in the contentious debates at St. Martin's Lane in the mid-1750s about

addition, virtually nothing is known about him: his name never surfaces in Vertue, Walpole, or in other chronicles of London's artistic scene, nor are there any other known publications credited to him.

167. For a profile of James Ralph, see E. Harris, *British Architectural Books and Writers, 1556–1785*, Cambridge, 1990, 381–85.

168. For the relation between Wilson and Hogarth, see Paulson, 62–63. Benjamin Ralph may well be a conflation of the names of James Ralph and Benjamin Wilson, and it is also worth noting in view of this era's penchant for word play that "Benjamin Ralph" and "Raphael Urbin" are almost (but not quite) anagrammatic.

169. S. H. A. Bruntjen, *John Boydell (1719–1804): A Study of Art Patronage and Publishing in Georgian London*, New York, 1985, 14–16.

170. It would seem more than mere coincidence that Richardson's *Account* (with its seventy-page encomium of Raphael) was published in a second edition in 1754, the same year the decision was made to flesh out *The School of Raphael* with additional plates.

171. The St. Martin's Lane Academy, originally set up in 1720 after the academy in Great Queen Street broke up (see n. 148), was an informal institution having neither official recognition nor a charter and was managed by a committee of sixteen elected artists and by a subcommittee who screened those who wanted to join.

how an academy should be organized. He took the position that an English institution should not be modeled on the French Royal Academy, but was challenged by Joshua Reynolds who was becoming increasingly influential at St. Martin's Lane and who found much to admire in the French system.[172] The clash between Hogarth and Reynolds was inevitable, given their polar personalities and their divergent views.[173] They may have agreed on the merit of Raphael's artistic genius, but they scarcely were swayed by the courtesy, tact, and good nature that Vasari lauded in the painters working in Raphael's studio.[174]

THE EXPRESSION OF THE PASSIONS

In his introduction to *The School of Raphael* the book's author shows his sympathy for one side of the partisan divide at St. Martins Lane by praising Hogarth (and Hogarth's ally Joshua Kirby),[175] but then he moves beyond artistic politics (ostensibly at least) to dwell upon what he regards as the profoundest part of painting: the *characteristics of the passions.* To this end the book challenges the reigning authority Charles Le Brun, the French painter who shaped the curriculum of the French Academy and whose posthumously published lecture on the passions enjoyed international prestige.[176] Considerable currency was given to Le Brun's ideas about the graphic depiction of the passions by André Félibien's published interpretation of Le Brun's painting *The Tent of Darius* (fig. 45), which was widely circulated in its English translation.[177] With the literal exactitude endemic to secretaries of the French Academy, Félibien meticulously described the expressive response of each figure in Le Brun's depiction. As they came down to the eighteenth century in their most popularized form, Le Brun's "passions" were codified into a set of nineteen plates that ranged from rapture to despair (figs. 46, 48, 50–52). Although the Cartesian theory from which his corpus sprang was not much regarded in England, nothing had yet replaced these useful illustrations, and innumerable re-engravings after his modeled heads, and after the various diagrams outlining these same expressions in profile and full face, continued to be compelling instructional guides.[178]

172. Paulson (191–92) detects Reynolds's voice in "The Plan for an Academy," a fifteen-page booklet submitted to the Dilettanti Society in 1755. Hogarth took issue with this plan, and by the time of its publication he had withdrawn from the St. Martin's Lane group. In 1754 Hogarth joined the Society of Arts, mistakenly thinking that its ideas were compatible with his own. The Society (for the Encouragement of the Arts, Manufactures and Commerce) was founded by William Shipley, and its artistic training was basically geared to industrial applications.

173. In two anonymously published letters in 1759 in the *Idler,* nos. 76 and 82, Reynolds ridiculed the ideas that Hogarth put forth in the *Analysis of Beauty* (1753).

174. G. Vasari, *Lives of the Most Eminent Painters, Sculptors, and Architects,* London, (1568) 1979, 2:914.

175. Hogarth arranged an invitation for Kirby to give three lectures on perspective at the St. Martin's Lane Academy; he was then made an honorary member (Paulson, 186). Hogarth's theoretical treatise the *Analysis of Beauty* and Kirby's *Dr. Brook Taylor's Method of Perspective Made Easy* (1754) stirred controversy because of their Lockean assumption that common judgment is based on custom and experience, not mathematical reason. Kirby's book was dedicated to Hogarth, who provided the engraved frontispiece. For a discussion of the reception of Kirby's book, see Harris, *British Architectural Books,* 254–58.

176. For the most comprehensive discussion of Le Brun's ideas, drawings, subsequent publications, and derivatives, see Montagu, *Expression of the Passions.*

177. *The Tent of Darius Explain'd,* 1703.

178. An example is the elaborate folding plate depicting twelve heads after Le Brun's *Expressions des Passions de l'ame* appeared in Robert Dodsley's *Preceptor* in 1748. The plate was engraved by Francis Hayman, a drawing master at the St. Martin's Lane Academy (B. Allen, *Francis Hayman,* exh. cat., Yale Center for British Art, New Haven, 1987, cat. no. 84).

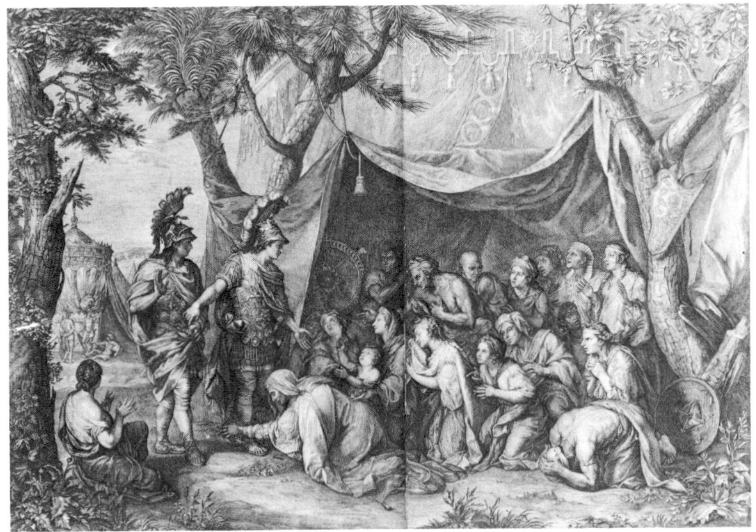

FIG. 45 Simon Gribelin (after Charles Le Brun), *The Tent of Darius*, 1693 (*cat. 8*)

Although Le Brun was the only one to have dealt comprehensively with the passions from the perspective of the painter, his work was seen as sorely deficient. In *The School of Raphael* he is mightily challenged by the authority of those "inimitable" Cartoons, which are recommended as a far richer source of study.

> A person who has only studied Le Brun, will be at a loss when he views some of the Characters in the Cartoons to know what Passions are expressed in them, and yet the ideas will be found to be in the highest degree, exalted, just, and significant; and he will be struck with astonishment and disgust, when he returns to his former study, in which he will find no traces to lead his Ideas back to the point from which they first set out.

One can appreciate the author's mischievous ploy of turning the passionate response "astonishment and disgust" back on Le Brun himself by likening it to the expression of contempt that Raphael (at least theoretically) has given to an Athenian youth listening to Paul's harangue.[179] Some years later Thomas Rowlandson continued this sport with a full-scale graphic send-up of Le Brun's passions (figs. 47, 49, 53–55). But the more serious point was that Raphael's sublime expressions were not legible according to the system Le Brun had devised.[180] His system focused on the eyebrows in consequence of their physical proximity to the pineal gland, which Descartes had located as the prime receptor of the passions of the soul. Le Brun's stress on the eyebrows as the expressive fulcrum of the face, and his detailed charting of their most dramatic movements, proved to be an effective guide to the emotional states displayed in his own paintings of tumultuous battles; but for Raphael, eyebrow movements were scarcely the lever for controlling the depiction of emotional states.

As the introduction to *The School of Raphael* demonstrates, the Cartoons played an ever more prominent role in English discussions of the physiognomy of the passions. At the same time, the language of that discourse shifted from the physiological terminology of Descartes

179. In the index to *The School of Raphael*, the most forward figure of the group—seated directly in front and pointing to Paul—is identified as expressing "astonishment with disgust"(pl. 20.2).

180. Heads from the Cartoons identified as illustrating acute pain, compassion, and terror (pls. 7.1, 2.2, 10.1&2) do not have the same pathognomic character as those by Le Brun in *Expressions des Passions de l'ame* (pls. 10, 14, 17).

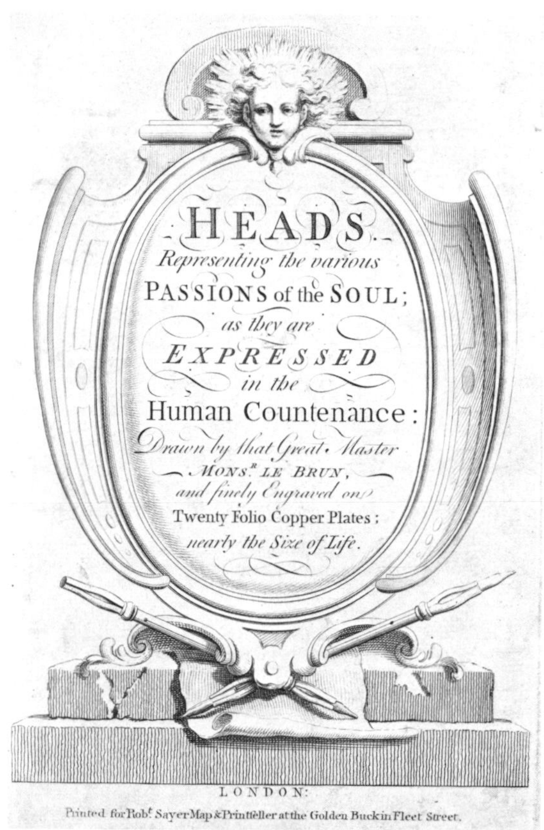

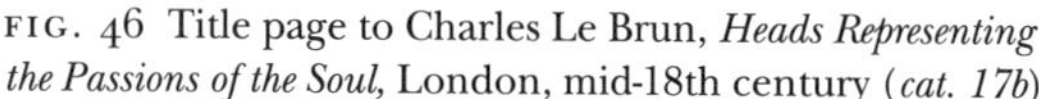

FIG. 46 Title page to Charles Le Brun, *Heads Representing the Passions of the Soul*, London, mid-18th century (*cat. 17b*)

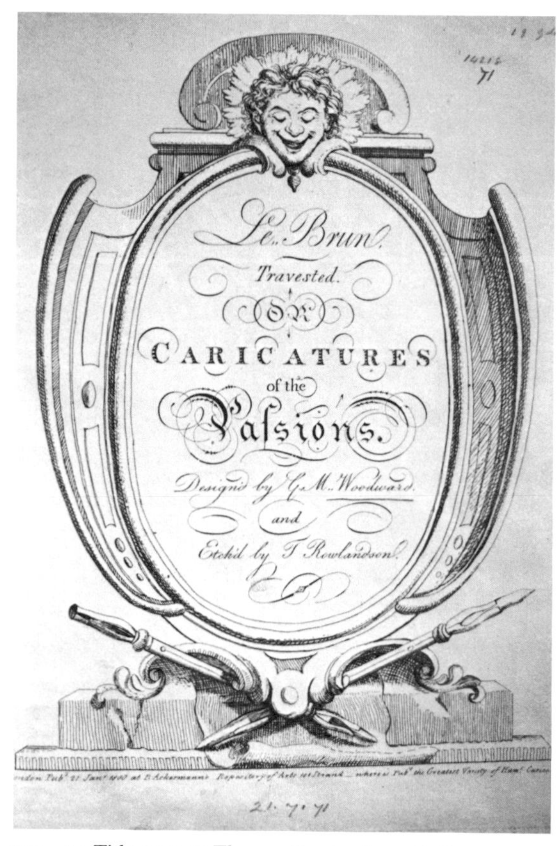

FIG. 47 Title page to Thomas Rowlandson, *Le Brun Travested or Caricatures of the Passions*, London, 1800

to the more psychological terminology of Francis Hutchinson, David Hume, and Adam Smith.[181] In the process, the high-minded content of the Cartoons was claimed to be virtually English in its moral sentiment. Here the "affections"–the term Hutchinson employed to distinguish pure and spiritual responses from violent confused sensations[182]–are within a narrow and temperate, and eminently "British," compass. Foremost in the Acts of the Apostles are the same expressions of curiosity, doubt, attention, astonishment, valor, celestial ardor, and compassion that Vasari found so admirable in the *Disputa* and *Transfiguration*.[183] Raphael's Cartoons moved the discussion of the passions out of the violent vocabulary of military conquest of Le Brun. The high emotions evinced in the battles and triumphs of Alexander that Le Brun painted for Louis XIV were upstaged by the radiance of Raphael's apostolic subjects. Decades earlier, noting that Raphael's angelic mind was a stranger to cruel and savage sentiment, Richardson advised that his works should be studied above all others.[184] The nobility and dignity of his characters were seen to raise the expressive significance

181. F. Hutchinson, *An Essay on the Nature and Conduct of the Passions and Affections with Illustrations on the Moral Sense*, 1728; D. Hume, *Essay on the Passions*, 1739; A. Smith, *The Theory of Moral Sentiments*, 1759.

182. Hutchinson, *An Essay*, 59, 69, notes the great confusion in terminology in treatises on the passions, and he also points out the important distinction that is often overlooked, i.e., the great difference between a private and a public affection.

183. Vasari, *Lives*, 2:889, 907–8. Vasari, however, only briefly mentions the Tapestry Cartoons, and primarily to marvel at the miraculous effect of the costly gold and silver threads used by the weavers in Flanders.

184. Richardson (1715) 1725, 114.

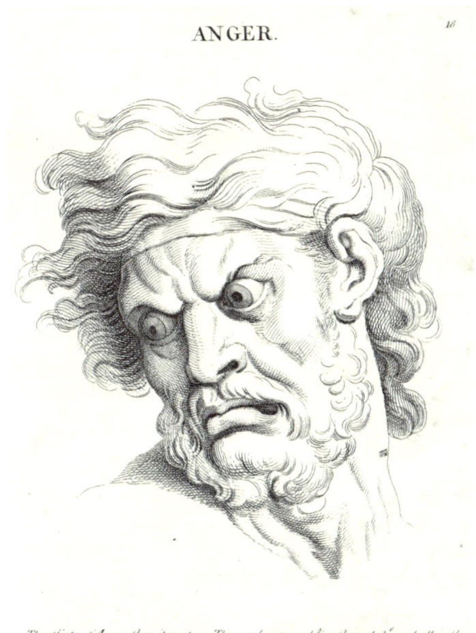

FIG. 48 *Anger*, in Charles Le Brun, *Heads Representing the Passions of the Soul*, mid-18th century (*cat. 17c*)

FIG. 49 *Anger*, in Thomas Rowlandson, *Le Brun Travested* (*cat. 26q*)

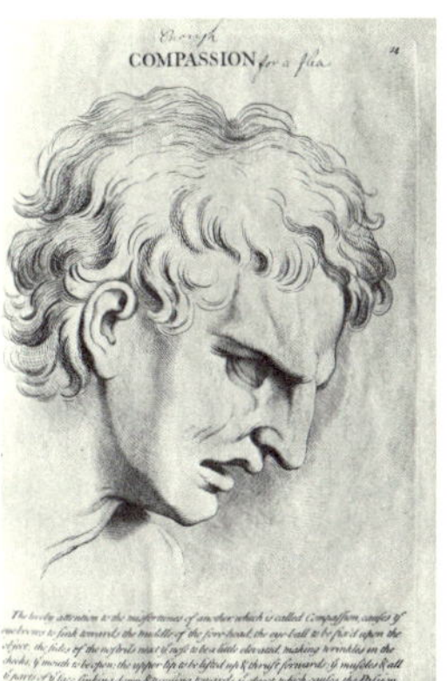

FIG. 50 *Compassion*, in Charles Le Brun, *Heads Representing the Passions of the Soul*, 1794

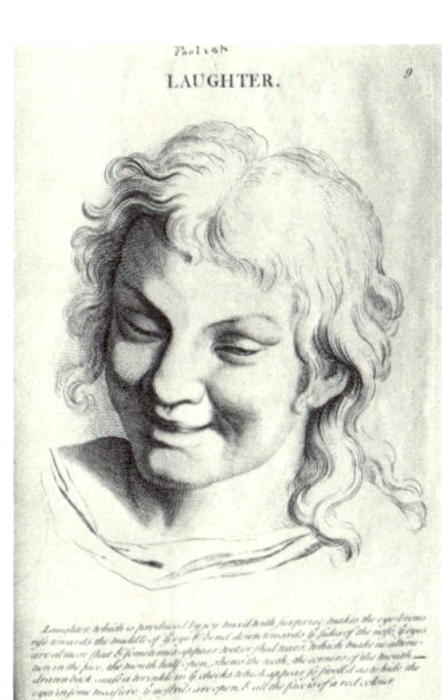

FIG. 51 *Laughter*, in Charles Le Brun, *Heads Representing the Passions of the Soul*, 1794

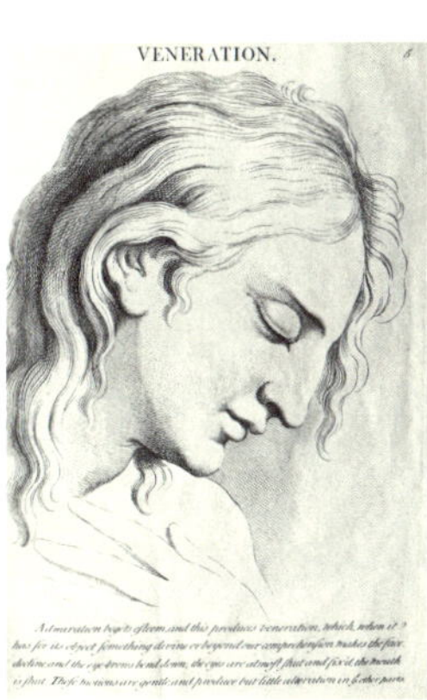

FIG. 52 *Veneration*, in Charles Le Brun, *Heads Representing the Passions of the Soul*, 1794

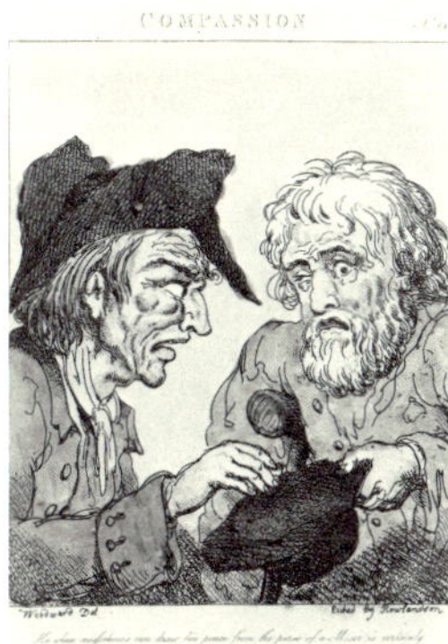

FIG. 53 *Compassion*, in Thomas Rowlandson, *Le Brun Travested* (*cat. 26m*)

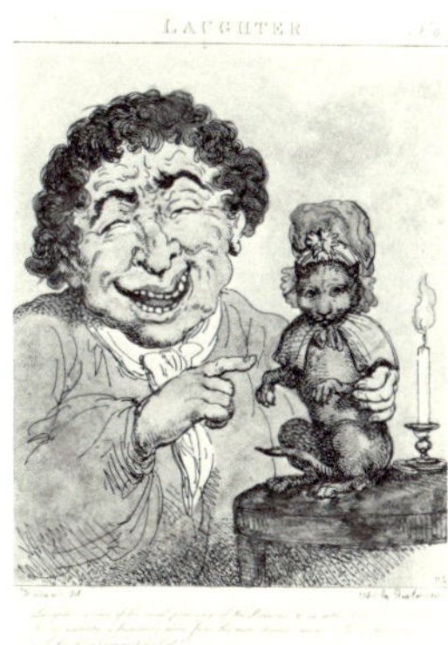

FIG. 54 *Laughter*, in Thomas Rowlandson, *Le Brun Travested* (*cat. 26h*)

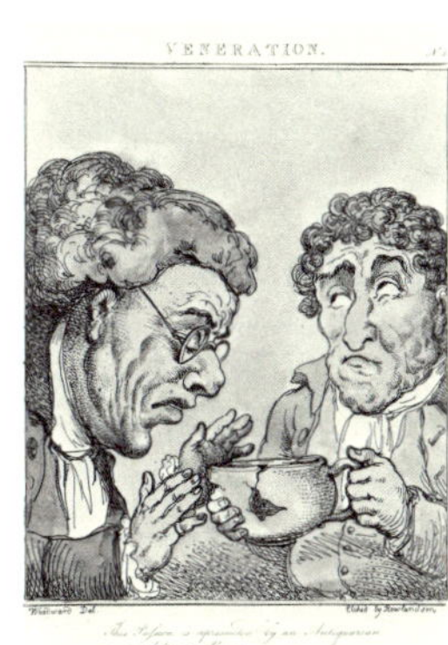

FIG. 55 *Veneration*, in Thomas Rowlandson, *Le Brun Travested* (*cat. 26d*)

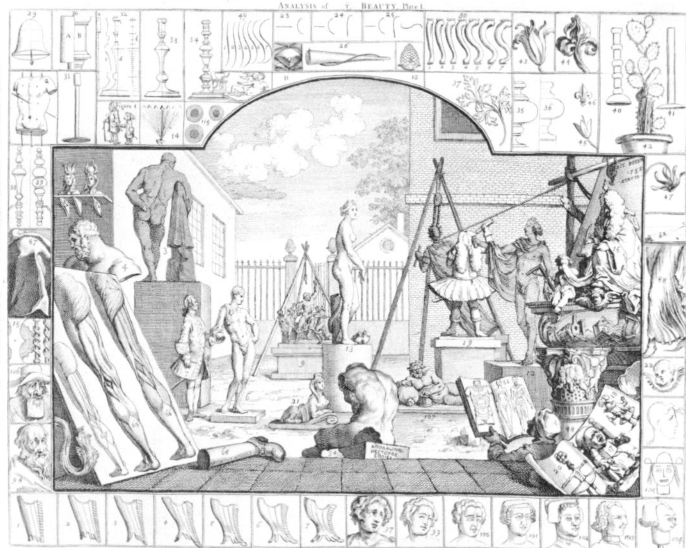

FIG. 56
William Hogarth, *Statuary Yard*, 1753, plate 1 in *Analysis of Beauty* (*cat. 12a*)

FIG. 56A, detail of fig. 56

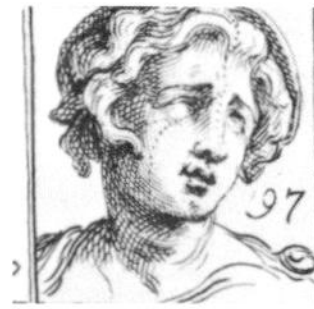

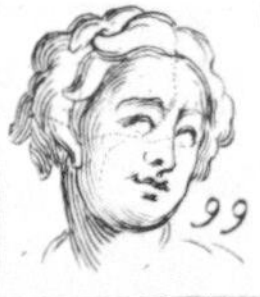

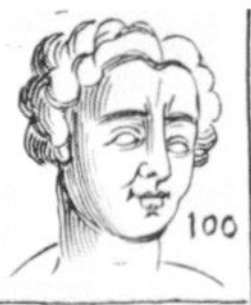

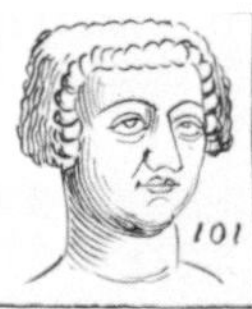

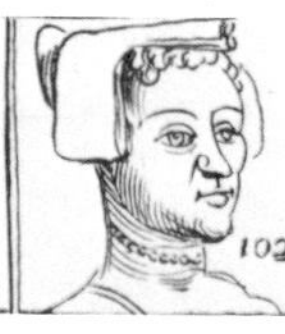

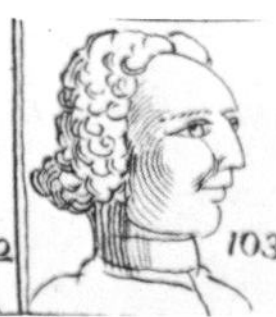

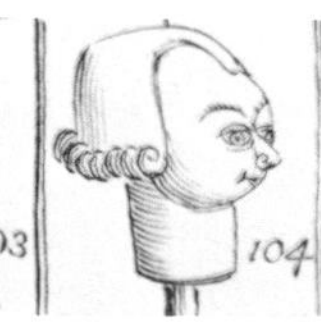

of the passions to the level of the sublime. By this curious route, the Hampton Court Cartoons were used to stake a British claim in the arena of the "expression of the passions," a terrain that the French had long guarded as sacred Cartesian ground. By looking directly to Hampton Court, England could bypass the French in mastering the language of narrative painting and–most especially–the nuances of expression.

A truly novel feature of *The School of Raphael* was the extensive alphabetical list of expressions that indexed each of the ninety heads. By expanding Le Brun's corpus of expressions from nineteen to fifty-three–by this multiplication and nuancing of the passions–it aimed to provide both a larger and better lexicon. Its broadened scope challenged Le Brun's precise rules by emphasizing the variety and degree of the passions.[185] In reality, the many shades of emotional response listed in the index for Raphael's various characters could never have been distinguished from one another. Reynolds, who denied the very possibility of expressing a "mixed passion," surely had this popular publication in mind when he addressed the issue in his fifth Discourse delivered at the Royal Academy:

> There are many writers on our art, who, not being of the profession, and consequently not knowing what can or cannot be done, have been very liberal of absurd praises in their descriptions of favorite works. They always find in them what they are resolved to find. They praise excellencies that can hardly exist together; and above all things are fond of

185. This was more in sympathy with the ideas of Roger de Piles, who rejected Le Brun's prescriptions and found the Ancients' appeal to nature more valuable. De Piles claimed one cannot give precise rules for the depiction of the passions, and he emphasized their variety and diversity. Also, he thought the eyes—not the eyebrows—were the site where the passions of the soul registered (*Cours de Peinture par Principes* (1708) reprint Geneva, 1969, 161–76). In a chart rating painters from 1 to 20 (following the "Balance des Peintres," ibid., 489–93), De Piles gave Raphael the highest mark for expression—that is, eighteen points, while he gave Le Brun sixteen.

FIG. 57
William Hogarth, *Paul before Felix*, 1752 (*cat. 11*)

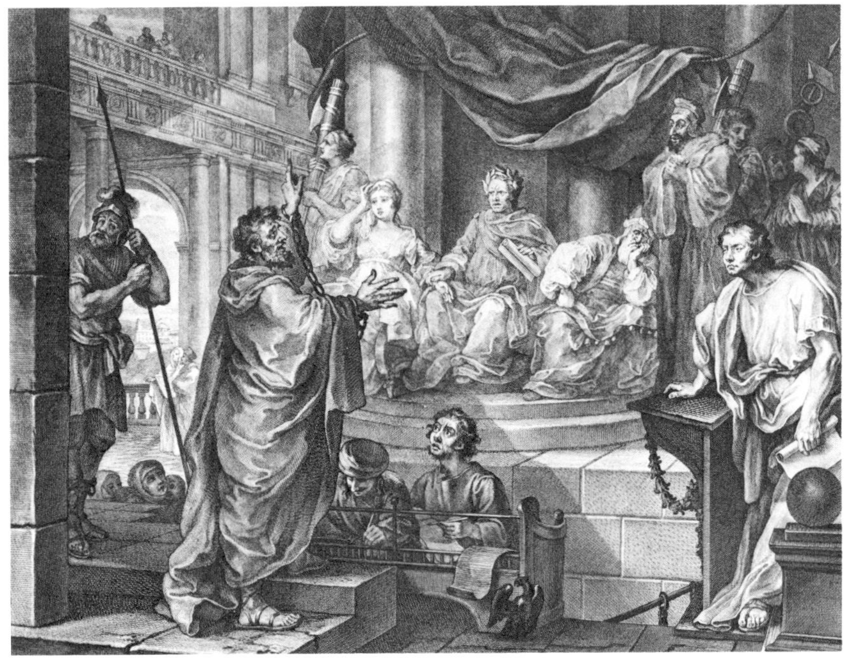

describing with great exactness the expression of a mixed passion, which more particularly appears to me out of the reach of our art.

Such are many disquisitions which I have read on some of the Cartoons and other pictures of Raffaelle, where the Criticks have described their own imaginations; or indeed where the excellent master himself may have attempted this expression of passions above the powers of the art; and has therefore, by an indistinct and imperfect marking, left room for every imagination, with equal probability to find a passion of his own.[186]

Despite the justness of such criticism, the intended aim of *The School of Raphael* was to rescue the study of emotions from the realm of a priori precepts and move it into the realm of natural observation. Noted in the book's preface was that some contemporary artists followed "nature" as Raphael had done, and that "a collection of the passions, as they are found in nature, might be made from the works of Mr. Hogarth which would do honor to that master and prove of great utility to young students."[187]

Hogarth's appreciation of Raphael certainly ran long and deep. In the *Analysis of Beauty* he cites Raphael's depiction of great men as an example of the highest taste; and in a plate illustrating the text, he shows a series of faces that progressively deviate from that ideal (figs. 56, 56a).[188] Evidence is also readily seen in the composition of his most blatant homage, *Paul before Felix* (fig. 57), as well as in the lower register of *Characters and Caricaturas* (figs. 58, 58a). In the latter Hogarth singles out three of the most memorable figures in the Cartoons: the lame man and the apostles Paul and John, paying tribute to Raphael as an excellent de-

186. Reynolds, 78–79.

187. In his *Analysis of Beauty* (1753), reprint Cambridge, 1955, 138, Hogarth recommends looking at the gamut of expressions ranging from tranquility to extreme despair in the common drawing book called *Le Brun's Passions of the Mind*, noting that while these are imperfect copies they are the best available because the passions are arranged in succession and distinctly marked with lines and no shadows.

188. Ibid., 134–36. Hogarth identifies face no. 97 (in the bottom border of pl. I) as the highest taste and nos. 99–106 as deviations from it.

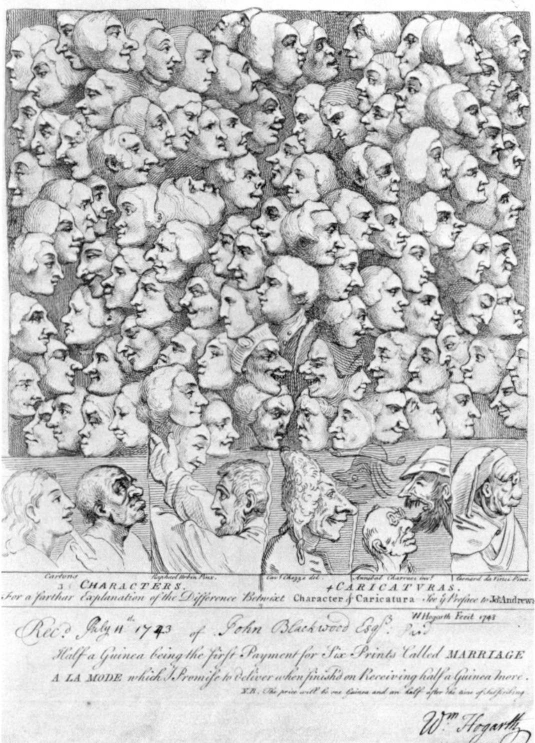

FIG. 58
William Hogarth, *Characters and Caricaturas*, 1743 (*cat. 10*)

FIG. 58A, detail of fig. 58

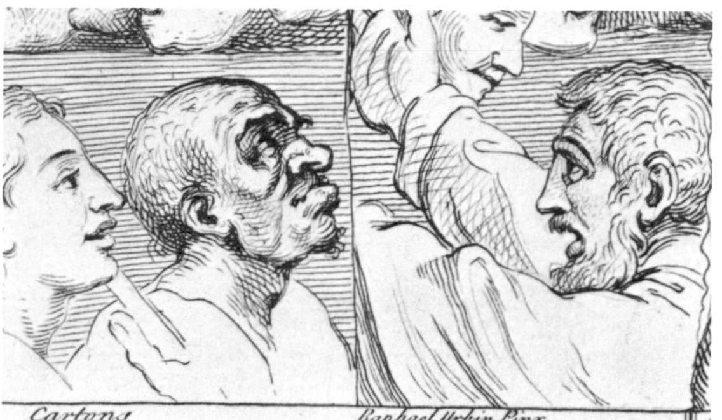

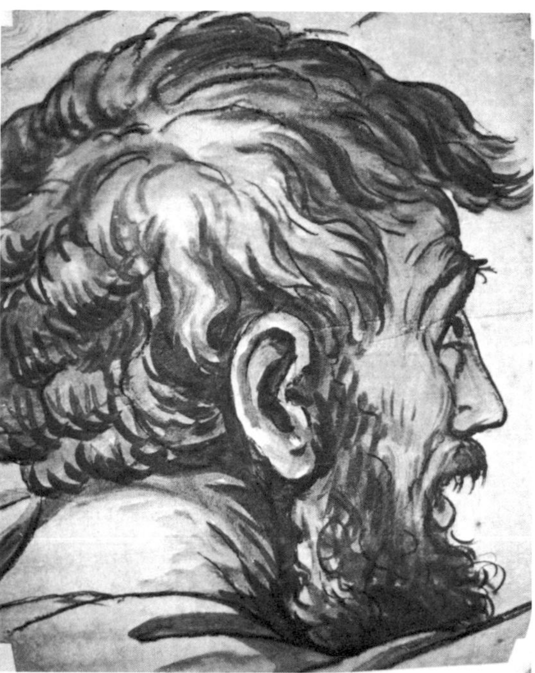

FIG. 59 James Thornhill (after Raphael), *Paul Preaching at Athens*, ca.1729, brush and brown ink, 14 x 10 in., from an album of tracings, Saint Paul's Cathedral, London

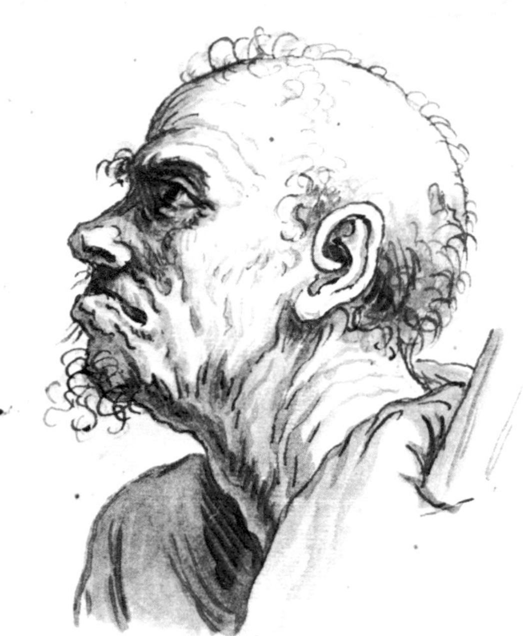

FIG. 60 James Thornhill (after Raphael), *Paul Preaching at Athens*, ca.1729–31 (*cat. 31*)

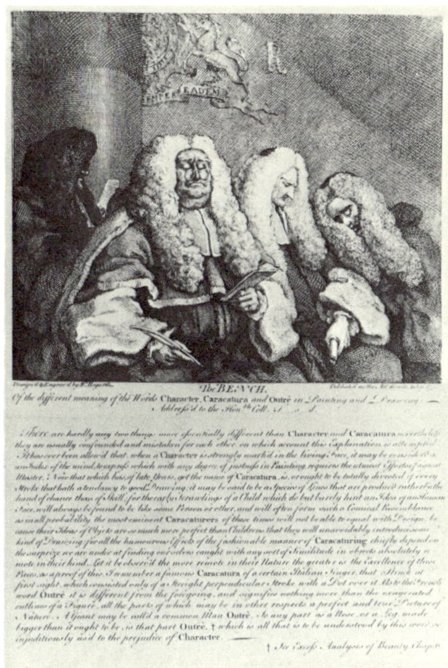

FIG. 61 William Hogarth, *The Bench*, 1st state, 1758 (*cat. 13*)

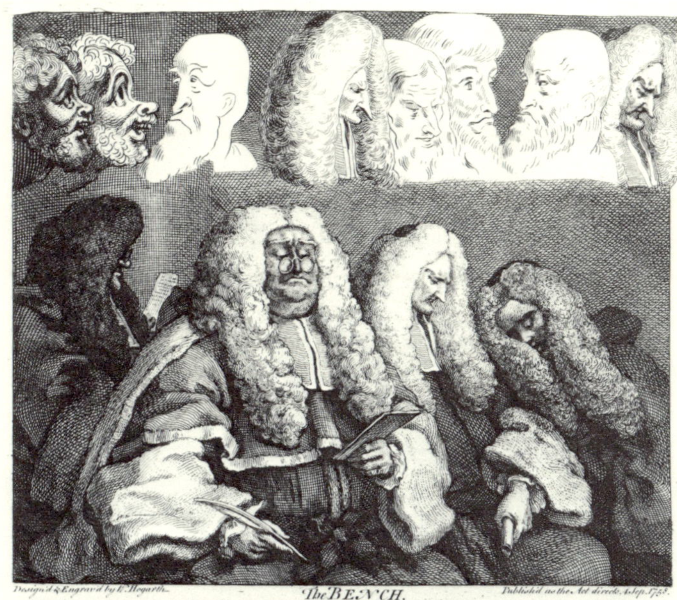

FIG. 61A William Hogarth, *The Bench,* 5th state, detail (1758), 1764 (*cat. 13a*)

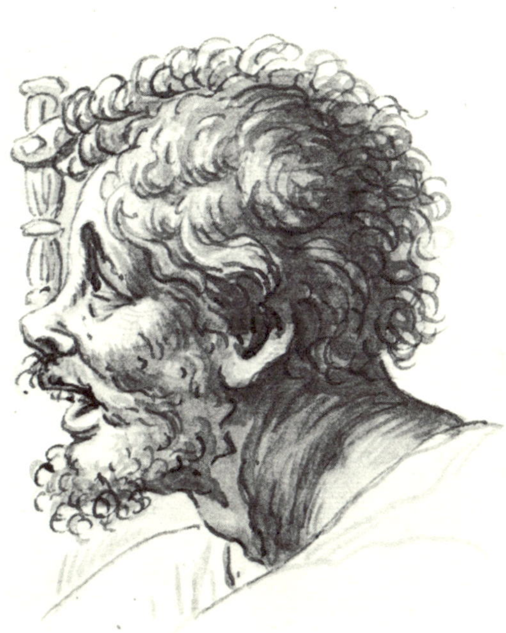

FIG. 62 James Thornhill (after Raphael), *The Sacrifice at Lystra,* ca.1729–31 (*cat. 31*)

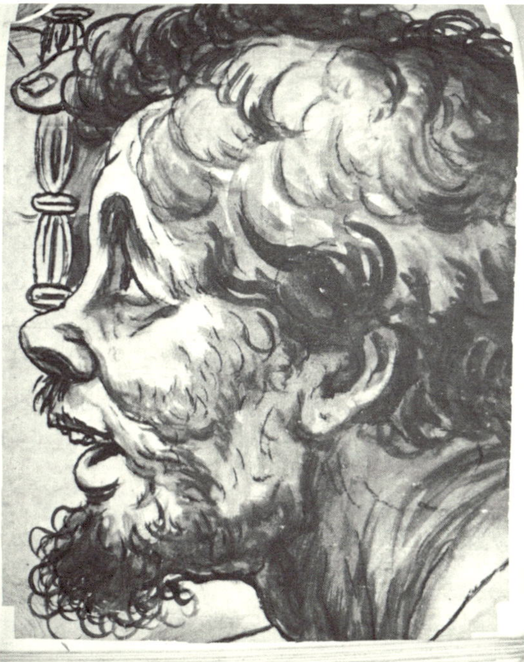

FIG. 63 James Thornhill (after Raphael), *The Sacrifice at Lystra,* ca.1729, brush and brown ink, 14 x 10 in., from an album of tracings, Saint Paul's Cathedral, London

lineator of character.[189] When some years later, he was still concerned to clarify graphically the distinction between *character* and *caricature*, Hogarth addressed the issue in *The Bench*, a plate that he was working on in 1764, the year he died. Here, too, Raphael is his point of reference. From the top of the plate, which he had begun in 1758 (fig. 61), he burnished out the royal coat of arms and etched anew a suite of heads, two of which are from the Cartoons (fig. 61A).[190] Such approbation clearly redresses the claim of his critics that Hogarth was boorishly irreverent toward the old masters.

It is of note, too, that Hogarth married Jane Thornhill in 1729, the same year his father-in-law began to copy the Hampton Court Cartoons. Hogarth had recently put aside engraving with an eye to becoming a history painter but evidently offered to assist with the engravings for Thornhill's planned drawing manual based on the Cartoons. It is difficult to imagine what that joint venture would have yielded; the closest we can come is an unfinished plate of four etched heads from *Elymas Struck with Blindness* (fig. 64). It was published by Hogarth's wife in 1781 (seventeen years after his death) and bears the following inscription:

> Mr Walpole in his Anecdotes of Painting, Vol. IV, p. 22, speaking of the Cartoons at Hampton Court, observes that Sir James Thornhill having made copious studies of the heads, hands and feet, intended to publish an exact account of the whole for the use of students: but his work has never appeared. As the present plate was found among others belonging to the late Mr. Hogarth, it is not impossible but that it might have been engraved by him for his father-in-law S.r James's intended publication.

No drawings of these heads are in the album of Thornhill's small ink sketches in the Victoria and Albert Museum, suggesting that they might have gone astray or perhaps even been destroyed in the course of etching the plate. Yet, large-scale tracings of them do exist in the larger Thornhill album (figs. 65, 66), and these are very close in spirit to Hogarth's etching. The relation between the plate and tracings is especially apparent when the expressive and bristly quality of both Thornhill's drawn and Hogarth's etched heads is compared with the slick rendering of those same faces by French engravers (fig. 35). Thornhill's lively drawings of Raphael's "heads" show that late in his career he was energized by a new interest in facial expression that replaced his earlier concern with figural arrangement and rhetorical gesture.

A brief addendum to the spin-off production of heads from Raphael's Cartoons is the stimulus it gave to other engravings of heads that were mined from Raphael's Vatican frescoes. Among these publications were the 180 heads, primarily from Raphael, etched by Paolo Fidanza, published in Rome in 1769 (fig. 69). This was followed by a handsome folio

189. In *Characters and Caricaturas* Hogarth visually illustrates Henry Fielding's argument in the preface to *Joseph Andrews* against caricature and burlesque as debased forms of character painting. Hogarth reproduces some of the caricatures published in England by Arthur Pond (after Ghezzi, Carracci, and Leonardo) in order to contrast them unfavorably with his own work and with Raphael's Cartoons. Hogarth's engraving is an angry response to the success of two sets of caricature prints that Pond published between 1736 and 1742 (for Pond's printselling activities, see L. Lippincott, *Selling Art in Georgian London: The Rise of Arthur Pond*, New Haven, 1983, 127–59.

190. One head is of the healed lame man in the *Sacrifice at Lystra*, the other is of the third apostle from the right in *Christ's Charge to Peter*. On the unfinished plate, one of his assistants has added, "this Plate would have been better expain'd had the Author lived a Week longer" (for Hogarth's prints see R. Paulson, *Hogarth's Graphic Works*, London, 1989).

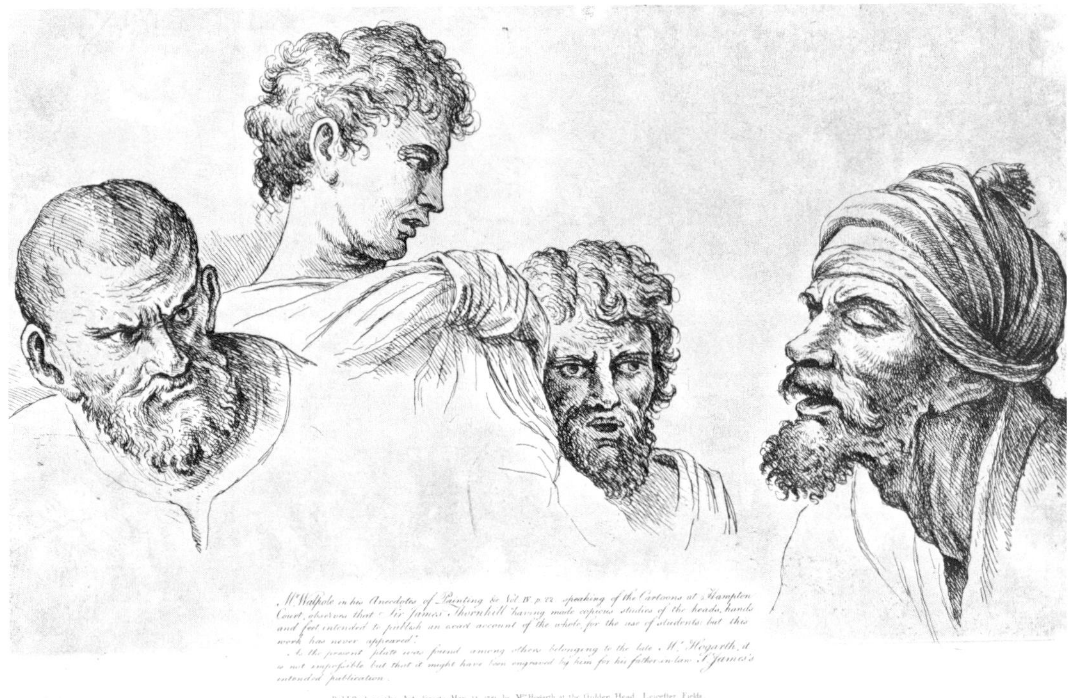

FIG. 64 William Hogarth (after Raphael), *Heads of Elymas and Three Men*, 1781 (*cat. 14*)

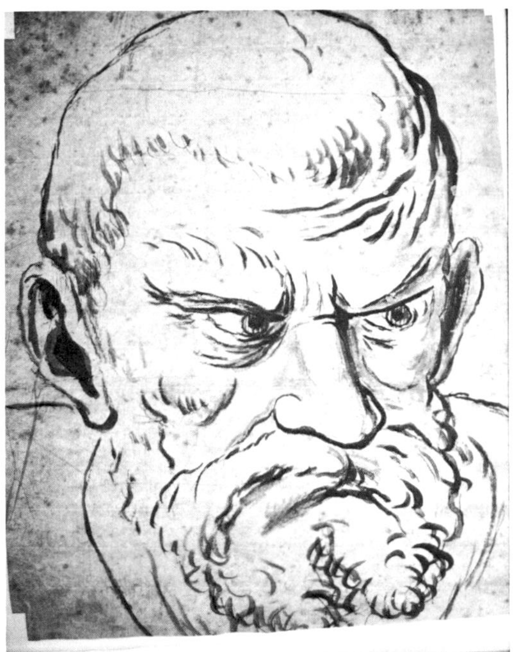

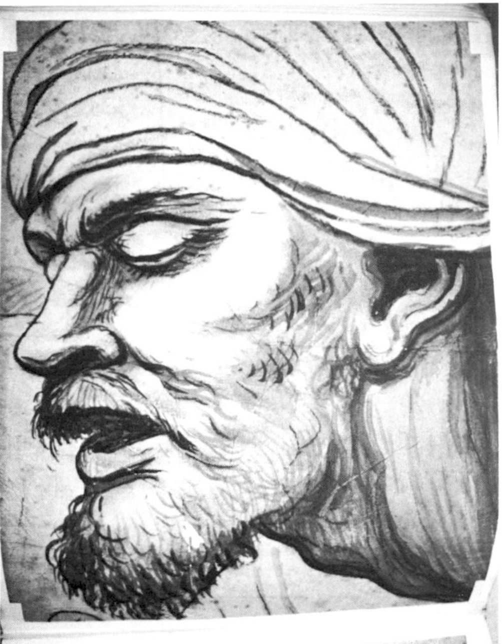

FIGS. 65 & 66 James Thornhill (after Raphael), *Elymas Struck with Blindness*, ca.1729, brush and brown ink, 14 x 10 in., from an album of tracings, Saint Paul's Cathedral, London

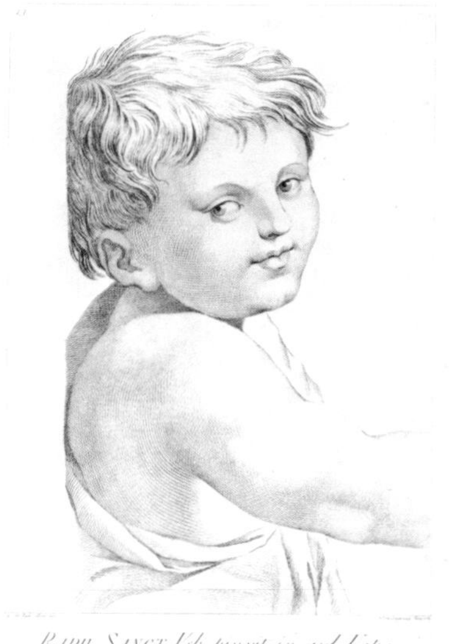

FIG. 67 Anton Raphael Mengs (after Raphael), Head of a Boy, engraved by Domenico Cunego, in *Le LII Teste della Celebre Scuola d'Atene . . .* , Rome, 1785 (*cat. 19*)

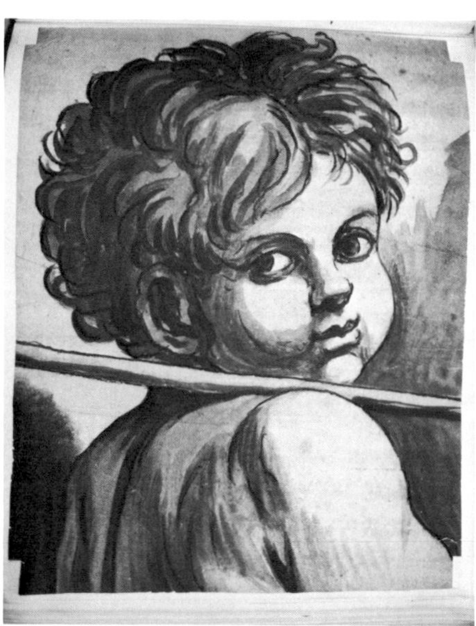

FIG. 68 James Thornhill (after Raphael), *The Lame Man Healed*, ca.1729, brush and brown ink, 14 x 10 in., from an album of tracings, Saint Paul's Cathedral, London

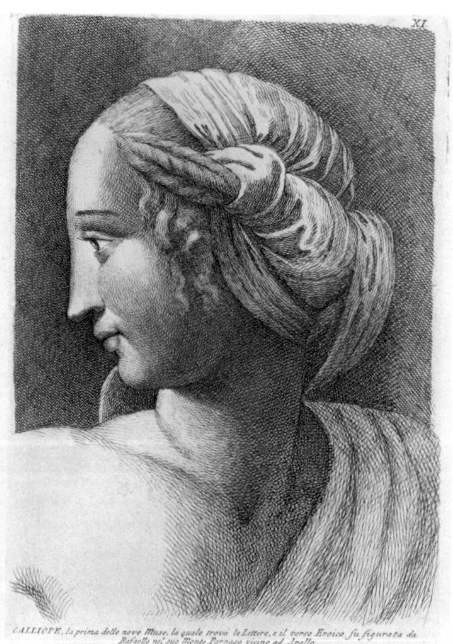

FIG. 69 Paolo Fidanza (after Raphael), Head of Calliope, in *Teste Scelte di Personaggi Illustri in Lettere, e in Armi, Cavate gia dall' Antico, o dall' Originale, e Dipinte nel Vaticano da Rafaello d'Urbino*, Rome, 1769

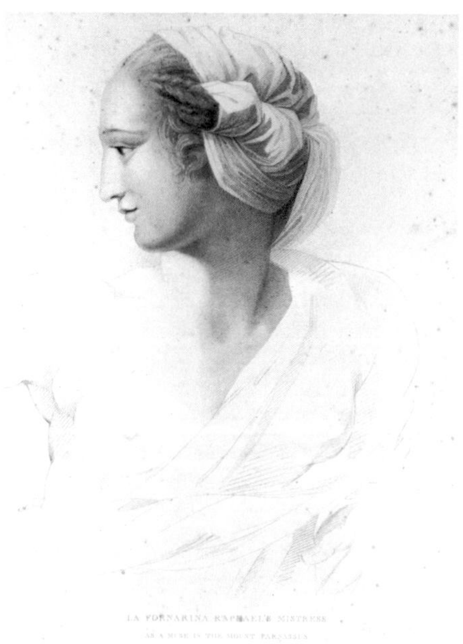

FIG. 70 R. Duppa (after Raphael), Head of La Fornarina, in *Heads from the Fresco Pictures of Raffaello in the Vatican*, London, 1802 (*cat. 5*)

edition of the 52 heads that Anton Raphael Mengs had traced from *The School of Athens* around 1746–49,[191] engraved by Domenico Cunego and posthumously published in 1785 (fig. 67).[192] But it is a London publication in 1802, *Heads from the Fresco Pictures of Raffaello in the Vatican* (fig. 70), that clearly augers the new century. A telling comparison with Fidanza's eighteenth-century plates is the now popular stipple engraving technique[193] which substantially softens the forms. Of interest, too, is that the head of Calliope–the most idealized muse in Raphael's *Parnassus*–has been personalized into his mistress, La Fornarina. Both the rendering and the identity signal a new idea of Raphael in the nineteenth century which was culled from his early devotional works and which savored of historical fiction.

V. RELIGIOUS SUBJECT MATTER OF THE CARTOONS

RELIGIOUS CLIMATE IN THE EARLY EIGHTEENTH CENTURY

IN LIGHT OF THE TORRENT of pietistic literature produced in England early in the eighteenth century, any account of Raphael's Acts of the Apostles must consider their religious content.[194] Although the eighteenth century continues to be popularly regarded as preeminently secular, that view has been losing ground as religious interests in general, and the Church's activities in particular, are increasingly shown to have played a more prominent role than has usually been assumed.[195]

The Cartoons appealed to the very special affection the English had for the apostle Paul, that zealous preacher whom some contended even Demosthenes could not vie with for sublime and pathetic eloquence.[196] And British Protestants could virtually discount the fact that Raphael's sacred histories were commissioned by a Roman Catholic pope.[197] They were con-

191. These may have been made in preparation for the copy of the *School of Athens* that Mengs painted in 1755 for Sir Hugh Smithson-Percy, first duke of Northumberland, for Northumberland House (see Roettgen, *Mengs e Raffaello*, 632 and n. 57).

192. Even granting that Cunego's engraving is at one remove from Mengs's original tracing, the vigor of Thornhill's tracing of a young boy (fig. 68) from *The Lame Man Healed* (fig. 3) is especially compelling in comparison with Mengs's listless image.

193. Regarding stipple engraving as a technique scorned by line engravers, see B. Dix, *Painting for the Parlour*, exh. cat., National Gallery of Ontario, Toronto, 1983, 19.

194. Little attention thus far has been paid to the reception of the Cartoons in terms of their theological content as compared with the copious discussions that have centered on their purely formal qualities. Formal considerations similarly have overshadowed theological content in discussions of the oratorio as a musical form (R. Smith, *Handel's Oratorios and Eighteenth Century Thought*, Cambridge, 1995), and of the sermon as the model of prose form (W. F. Mitchell, *English Pulpit Oratory from Andrewes to Tillotson: A Study of Its Literary Aspects*, London, 1932).

195. J. Barry, "Cultural Patronage and the Anglican Crisis," in Walsh, 191ff., and J. Gregory, "Anglicanism and the Arts: Religion, Culture and Politics in the Eighteenth Century," in *Culture, Politics and Society in Britain, 1660–1800*, Manchester, 1991, 82–109.

196. D. Longinus, *On the Sublime*, trans. W. Smith, London, 1739, xvii. The linkage between eloquence and the sublime made Paul preaching the ideal subject for the frontispiece of T. Gibbons, *Rhetoric*, London, 1767, and for the frontispiece to Longinus (figs. 74,75).

197. On the other hand, Raphael's paintings also would have had great appeal for Non-Jurists, since they were the true Catholic remnant in England and thus would have been most sympathetic to the notion of religious painting. Non-Jurists subscribed to the idea of a divine appointment of a hereditary monarch and, thus having sworn an oath to James II, would not swear a new oath to William and Mary. Although the Non-Jurists detested Lutherans and the Reformed Church, they nonetheless were utterly opposed to Rome (Rupp, 6).

vinced that these scripturally pure and truthful narratives traced the origin of the Protestant faith and, therefore, regarded their content as more in accord with the Church of England than with the Church of Rome. Called upon by Anglican divines, politicians, and poets, Raphael's apostles became truly naturalized in eighteenth-century England when they became engaged in the critical discourse about religious subject matter and the nature of the sublime.

While only those with access to Hampton Court would have seen the original Cartoons in this era, the general public had been made familiar with Raphael's expressive figures by frequent descriptions heard from the pulpit or read in the press. Richard Steele, for instance, stirred the passions of his audience with verbal images of *Elymas Struck with Blindness* and *The Death of Ananias* in 1711[198] and a few years later invoked Raphael's *Christ's Charge to Peter* in defense of the majesty of Holy Scripture.[199] Clerics also drew from the same deep well: Bishop Hoadly's sermons often presented the apostle Paul as the preacher's surrogate,[200] and a pithy poetic tribute to the Bishop of Rochester likened him to Paul as Raphael had depicted him at Athens.[201]

When the Cartoons first were installed at Hampton Court, not long after William III signed the Act of Toleration (1689),[202] the perennial Anglican concern was to return to the undivided primitive Church. But while political and ecclesiastical strife plagued the reigns of both William III and Queen Anne, on the positive side these were also times of religious revival and renewal.[203] By 1710, some forty-two societies had been founded to strengthen religious life,[204] and this trend was accompanied by an outpouring of pamphlets and books promoting (and opposing) the Book of Common Prayer. As the prayer book became a major item of debate, some advocates of liturgical change looked to the Apostolic Constitutions in hope of returning to the practices of the early Church.[205]

> The liturgy of the Apostolic Constitutions is the most ancient Christian liturgy extant: that it is perfectly pure and free from interpolation: and that the book itself called the Apostolic Constitutions contains at large the doctrines, laws and settlements which the three first and purest ages of the gospel did with one consent believe, obey and submit to and that as derived from Apostolic men.[206]

198. The *Spectator*, no. 227, 19 November 1711 (see above p. 28).

199. The *Guardian*, no. 21, 4 April 1713.

200. "*Epistle to the Romans, XIII: 1,* a sermon preached before the Lord Mayor and Court of Aldermen of the City of London 1704"; and "*Saint Paul's Behavior towards the Civil Magistrate,* a sermon preach'd at the Assizes at Hertford, 26 July 1708."

201. "So ATHENS once upon her Preacher hung,/Transported by the Precepts of his Tongue:/So stood great PAUL; so skillful RAPHAEL drew;/And as in Him another PAUL we view;/Another RAPHAEL may we find in you" (*Public Advertiser,* 3 January 1723/4).

202. The Act of Uniformity of 1662 had sown the seeds of dissent by excluding Presbyterians, Baptists, independents, and smaller sects from membership in the National Church. This was rectified by the Act of Toleration which exempted Protestant Nonconformists from all penalites to which religious dissidents had been liable and allowed them to have their own preachers and to meet for worship.

203. Henry Crompton, Lord Bishop of London, initiated a series of pastoral conferences in the 1690s in an attempt to renew the church. See J. Spurr, "The Moral Revolution of 1688" in Walsh, 128, and Rupp, 48–49.

204. The Society for the Reformation of Manners, The Society for the Promotion of Christian Knowledge (SPCK), among others; see C. Rose, "The Origins and Ideals of the SPCK 1699–1716," and Spurr, "The Moral Revolution of 1688," in Walsh, 172, 127.

205. See R. C. D. Jasper, *The Development of the Anglican Liturgy, 1662–1980,* London, 1989, 12. The Apostolic Constitutions, a collection of instructions relating to Chrisitan ecclesiastical practices, are based on the Teaching of the Apostles. They were composed after the death of the apostles, in the second century and later, when their teachings began to acquire infallable authority.

206. Thomas Deacon, 1734, quoted by Rupp, 23.

The turn toward the apostolic age—that formative and inspirational period when Christianity became a new independent religion—was a search for moral precepts and for an authoritative source of unifying religious belief. The Acts and the Gospels from which the narratives of Raphael's Cartoons derive are, along with the Epistles of Paul, the richest literary sources of the early history of the Church. There had been no precedent for depicting the stories of those messianic times on such a formidable scale, and Raphael's paintings virtually became as authoritative as the biblical text.

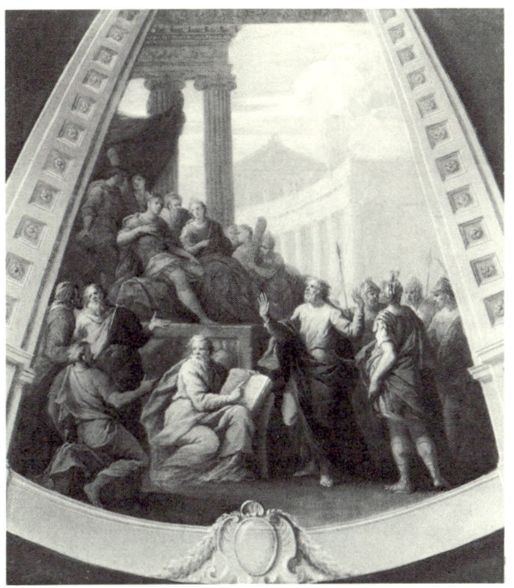

FIG. 71 James Thornhill, *Paul before Agrippa*, ca.1710 (*cat. 28*)

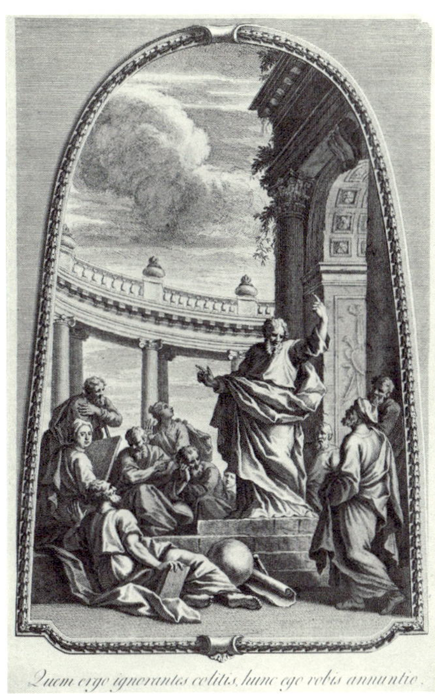

FIG. 72 James Thornhill, *Paul Preaching at Athens*, ca.1720, engraved by Gerard Vandergucht (*cat. 29f*)

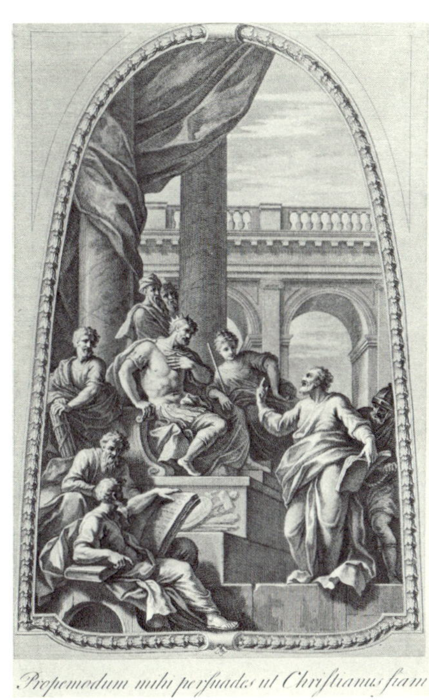

FIG. 73 James Thornhill, *Paul before Agrippa*, ca.1720, engraved by Charles Simonneau (*cat. 29c*)

THORNHILL'S APOSTLES AT SAINT PAUL'S AND THE TAPESTRY CARTOONS

By virtue of their subject matter, Raphael's Cartoons were especially relevant to the discussion about the nature of sacred imagery and the propriety of its use in the Protestant Church. In 1707 this became an urgent issue when, in the last stages of the completion of Wren's rebuilding of Saint Paul's, a decision had to be made about the nature of the decoration for the cupola. The sequence of events that ultimately led to Thornhill's commission to paint eight scenes in grisaille illustrating the Life of Saint Paul has recently been reconstructed by Carol Gibson-Wood. She argues convincingly that the ever-changing plans had more to do with the political composition of successive building committees—that is, with whether High Church or Low Church attitudes prevailed—than it did with artistic intrigue and jockeying for reputation, as has formerly been assumed.[207]

Though the Building Committee of the Royal Commission, appointed to oversee the rebuilding of Saint Paul's, seems to have had little enthusiasm for Wren's initial proposal to decorate the cupola in mosaic,[208] it can be surmised from the records that by 1708 he was authorized by the committee (of which he himself was a member) to allow Laguerre to begin preparing designs. These presumably were polychrome figural compositions somewhat along the lines of the first oil sketches that Thornhill prepared in hope of landing the commission (fig. 71). In 1709, however, after the Whigs swept into power in the general elections, the composition of the committee changed, and its voice grew more cautious. Minutes of its meetings reveal the committee's uncertainty about whether the dome should be painted with or without figures. They also show that the committee's attitude toward religious painting was that of Low Church sympathizers, who were eager to maintain a clear distinction between the Church of England and the Church of Rome. It is not that Whig bishops in general, or those on the committee, were staunchly opposed to religious painting; Anglican guidelines did allow depiction of instructionally rational, sacred histories. The committee merely drew the line on idolatrous, devotional works and the use of "divine machinery." Its vacillation about the decoration of Saint Paul's cupola points up how closely religion was tied to party politics, and how painting was in service to both. William Hayley's poetic reference to a "shaking Dome" offers a particularly apt description of this dispute in Queen Anne's reign:

> Tho' in suceeding years the Muses taught,
> "How *Ann* commanded, and how Marlbro' fought;"
> And *Thornhill's* blaze of Allegory gilt
> The piles, that *Wren's* superior genius built;
> Contending Factions, in her closing reign,
> Like winds imprison'd, shook fair Freedom's Fane.
> Painting, soft timid Nymph, still chose to roam,
> And fear'd to settle in this shaking Dome.[209]

The church clearly aimed to steer a middle, latitudinarian course, one that appealed to reason, common sense, and prudence. The imagery of the cupola was expected to match the message from the pulpit in proclaiming that the laws of God were reasonable. In England, as in other Protestant countries, religious subject matter was a more sensitive issue for painting than for poetry. Most argued that the human passions were more strongly moved by

207. Gibson-Wood 1993, 229–37, challenges the earlier account given by Croft-Murray, 1:71–74. My account is indebted to her interpretation of the politics of the commission.

208. It was probably considered too expensive, too lengthy in execution, and it would have required importing artists (Gibson-Wood 1993, 230).

209. "A Poetical Epistle to an Eminent Painter," 1778 (Chadwyck–Healy, English Poetry Full–Text Database [EPFTD], 1994).

forceful graphic representation than by verbal evocation, and therefore visual imagery was thought to be far more dangerous. Nonetheless, by considered maneuvers, the Church of England managed to position itself equidistant from Puritanism and Rome.

The Building Committee's decision in 1709 that the cupola's subject matter be confined to scriptural history and that the subjects be taken from the Acts of the Apostles must have been at least partially underwritten by the authority of the Cartoons at Hampton Court. Representations of the apostles could be seen as a very Protestant idea; Joseph Addison had wondered during his Italian sojourn of 1701–3 why "Roman Catholics, who are for this kind of worship, don't generally address themselves to the Holy Apostles, who have a more unquestionable right to the title of saints than those of a modern date; but these are at present quite out of fashion in Italy."[210]

It was at the same meeting in 1709 that a competition for the cupola design was announced that in effect revoked Laguerre's commission. It is not certain whether his designs were thought substantively or stylistically tainted by baroque associations (since no known designs survive), or whether it was thought Wren had too much say about an iconographic program that ought to be under clerical jurisdiction. In any event, by 1710 the competition had narrowed down to Thornhill and Pellegrini. The final decision was not taken until 1715 when a new board was appointed and Thornhill was unequivocally awarded the commission.[211] With Thornhill's appointment the prime conditions stipulated by one of the most vocal committee members, Archbishop Tenison, were finally satisfied: "I am no judge of painting, but on two articles I think I may insist: first that the painter employed be a Protestant; And, secondly, that he be an Englishman."[212]

Thornhill's cupola designs were almost inevitably influenced by Raphael's treatment of the same subject.[213] The Cartoons were physically close at hand and Thornhill had few if any other models of depictions of the Acts.[214] The Committee's stipulation that the cupola paintings were to be rendered in grisaille–that is, painted monochromatically and in a manner simulating sculptural reliefs–in effect leached papal associations from the subject matter. In Thornhill's translation,[215] Raphael's apostle's were rendered "English," in compliance

210. *Remarks on Several Parts of Italy, in the years 1701, 1702, 1703*, London, 1705, 30. Addison clearly left Italy too soon. By 1703 Pope Clement XI had plans well under way for the largest sculptural commission of the century, which was to fill the twelve large niches of the nave of Saint John Lateran with marble statues of the apostles. More surprising is that Richardson made no mention of the statues in 1722, although his son did visit the church in 1720/1 by which time most of the statues were finished (F. Den Broeder, "The Lateran apostles," *Apollo*, May 1967, 360–65).

It is somewhat ironic that Thornhill's apostles in Saint Paul's have a greater stylistic affinity with the statues in the Lateran (for which Carlo Maratta provided preliminary designs) than with Raphael's leaner and sparer classicism.

211. Pellegrini had left for Dusseldorf two years earlier, in 1713.

212. This often repeated comment was published in *Gentleman's Magazine*, LX, 1790, 992, but the original source was not given. The reader is referred to a note in the 1786, 6-volume edition of the *Tatler*, 4:275, but that source simply quotes from a notice in the *Weekly Packet* (no. 155, 25 June 1715) to the effect that the Commissioners agreed to have Thornhill paint the cupola and that he will "put to silence all the loud applauses hitherto given to foreign artists."

213. The unpublished dissertation by W. R. Osmun (the only full-scale study of Thornhill to date—see n. 126) offers a traditional inventory of possible sources for each of the cupola paintings, including Raphael, Rubens, A. Carracci, Le Sueur, and Sublyeras among others.

214. G. Waagen, *Works of Art and Artists in England*, London, 1838, 2:90. The program of Raphael's Acts of the Apostles, as of other great papal commissions, has been difficult to unravel; see C. F. Lewine, "Aries, Taurus, and Gemini in Raphael's *Sacrifice at Lystra*," *Art Bulletin*, LXXIII, June 1990, 271–83 (and forthcoming studies by the author).

with Shaftesbury's advice that painters mortify their colors when painting the apostles—that these poor simple men not be given the colorful and modern garb of lords or princes as in some contemporary portrayals.[216] More significantly, with the completion of Thornhill's paintings at Saint Paul's, the apostles were returned to a sacred setting.

RELIGIOUS POETRY AND THE SUBLIME

While the Cartoons were a benchmark of acceptable scriptural representation, they were also sometimes championed by zealous poets, like Richard Blackmore, whose pulpit perspective saw the road to Parnassus running straight through Jerusalem. Blackmore produced a lengthy poetic tribute to the Cartoons when he had the privilege of an assigned room at Hampton Court as physician in ordinary to William III. This he published anonymously in 1703, under the title *A Hymn to the Light of the World. With a short description of the Cartons of Raphael Urbin, in the Gallery at Hampton-court.* The longest homage was devoted to the most didactic of Raphael's subjects—*Paul Preaching at Athens*—and an excerpt gives indication of why Blackmore is mentioned more often by his enemies than by his friends.[217] Alas, no equivalent of Raphael's grace is to be found in his cumbersome couplets.

> Paul shews such great Concern, such sacred Awe,
> As if the Heav'nly Majesty he saw,
> By whose supream Commission he was sent,
> To treat with Rebel Man, and bring him to repent.
> Only that Preacher can th'Affections touch,
> Who's so in earnest, and whose Zeal is such.[218]

Such topical references were common practice in the eighteenth-century press, and while tributes to Raphael number in the hundreds, their literary merit rarely rises above the level of John Whaley's "Hail! ye fair Piles of *Hampton's* happy Groves,/Which *Raphael's* Works adorn, and *Brunswick* loves."[219]

If Blackmore's poetry was unconvincing as an argument for the religious transformation of poetry, there were others who made that plea far more effectively. John Dennis, Isaac Watts, and Aaron Hill were similarly impassioned champions of religious poetry, who, like Blackmore, saw the choice of the English Hercules as one between Christian virtue and pagan vice.[220] From their quarter there came innumerable poetic outpourings aspiring to the religious sublime.

It was through religious poetry that the notion of the sublime gained an aesthetic

215. Thornhill's set of grisaille oil sketches for the cupola are presently at the Tate Gallery. The British Museum has a great many preparatory studies for the cupola design as well as drawings Thornhill prepared for engravers. One such monochromatic study in gouache, marked to be engraved by Simmoneau, is at the Indianapolis Museum of Art.

216. A. A. Cooper, third earl of Shaftesbury, "A Notion of the Historical Draught of Tablature of the Judgment of Hercules" (1713), *Characteristics*, 1737, 2:372–73. Thornhill similarly noted during a trip to France in 1716/7 that the red, yellow, and white draperies of the apostles in Poussin's painting *Christ's Charge to Peter* were all too bright (MS. Notebook, Victoria and Albert Museum, Box 86.EE.87, f.89).

217. S. Johnson, *Lives of the English Poets*, London, 1854, 2:254.

218. Following this poetic homage to Raphael, Blackmore continued his applause in an essay "The Parallel between Poetry and Painting," published in the *Lay Monastery* in 1714.

219. *A Collection of Poems*, London, 1732, 287.

220. D. B. Morris, *The Religious Sublime: Christian Poetry and Critical Tradition in Eighteenth-Century England*, Louisville, KY, 1972, 83. See this source for a full discussion of the subject.

foothold in eighteenth-century England. Longinus may have provided the critical and aesthetic basis for the admiration of emotional religious verse and of biblical style, but it was John Dennis—the first English critic to make sublimity the fulcrum of his poetics—who led the way in advocating religious verse as a means of improving modern poetry. Dennis was unfazed by Longinus's silence on the relation between sublimity and religious ideas, finding in Milton's *Paradise Lost* proof enough that "religion in poetry was absolutely necessary to raise it to the greatest exultation of which so noble an art is capable."[221] Dennis was an earlier and more vocal devotee of Milton than either Addison or Richardson had been, and it was Dennis who made Milton and Longinus as inseparable to eighteenth-century readers as the starry twins, Castor and Pollux.

Those who sanctioned religious subject matter in poetry and in painting did not begin with a priori arguments on the nature of either of these arts. Rather, the starting points for both were the concrete examples of Milton's *Paradise Lost* and Raphael's Acts of the Apostles. The arguments for poetry made by John Dennis, Richard Blackmore, Isaac Watts, and Aaron Hill ran parallel to those made for painting by Joseph Addison, Richard Steele and Jonathan Richardson.

The general consensus about the sublimity of the works of Milton and Raphael seemed assurance enough that religious subject matter served the highest aesthetic and moral ends. Painting was at some disadvantage, since no native English artists loomed as large as Shakespeare or Milton, but some critics argued it superior as a medium of religious expression. Steele for one, writing in support of Dorigny's project to engrave the Cartoons, took the occasion to argue not only for religious subject matter but for the superiority of visual images over language, claiming that they more forcefully expressed the religious mind.[222] The highest compliment indeed that could be paid to an English painter was to dub him Raphael's successor,[223] a claim that was frequently made for Thornhill, as Dr. Young, for example, hyperbolically declared: "How Raphael's pencil lives in Thornhill's hand."[224] Another tribute to Thornhill's artistic performance at Saint Paul's was unsigned but no less enthusiastic:

221. Ibid., 56, quoted from *The Grounds of Criticism in Poetry* (1704). It is also worth noting that the preface, written by William Smith, to the most popular English translation of Longinus (1739) is replete with Christian references.

222. See above p. 28 and n. 42. He also argued for religious subject matter in the *Guardian (*no. 21, 4 April 1713) when he rallied support for Dr. Tillotson's contention that Virgil's descriptions of the Elysian Fields and the Infernal Regions were trifling by comparison with the majesty of Holy Scripture. Citing Raphael's painting *Christ's Charge to Peter* as proof of Tillotson's assertion, Steele claimed that Tillotson did not advance the idea merely in the service of his office as a clergyman, and then elaborated on the beneficial effects of viewing such religious art.

> When I look upon *Raphael's* Picture of our Saviour appearing to his Disciples after his Resurrection, I cannot but think the just Disposition of that Piece has in it the Force of many Volumes on the Subject: The Evangelists are easily distinguished from the rest by a passionate Zeal and Love which the Painter has thrown in the Faces; the Huddle group of those who stand most distant are admirable Representations of Men abashed with their late Unbelief and Hardness of Heart. And such Endeavours, as this of Raphael, and of all men not called to the Altar, are Collateral Helps not to be despised by the Ministers of the gospel.

223. William Kent was encouraged by his patron Burrell Masssingberd to become a second Raphael: "I have nothing to add but to beg you'll study and not think of coming over *donec Raphael Scundus eris*" (M. I. Wilson, *William Kent: Architect, Designer, Painter, Gardener, 1685–1748*, London, 1984, 12–13); and John Gay paid Kent a similar compliment in "Epistle IV: dedicated to The Right Honorable Paul Methuen Esq.": "There on the walls let thy just labours shine,/And Raphael live again in thy design." (Chadwyck–Healy, English Poetry Full–Text Database [EPFTD], 1994.

224. J. Hutchins, *History and Antiquities of Dorset,* 2:463.

Masterly touches—patient strokes of Art,
There Life awakes, there breathing *Pictures* start,
Or calmly Reason, or with Passion glow,
Or Preaching, seem with Eloquence to flow:
Most noble Sketches of thy skillful *Hand,*
Tints of thy *Pencil,*—Proof of thy command,
Immortal THORNHILL! mimick Life thy Play,
Second RAPHAEL, sacred Son of DAY![225]

Although nowadays the notion of the sublime in painting is typically associated with a taste for the terror of alpine landscape that emerged in the second half of the eighteenth century,[226] in the early decades when Jonathan Richardson addressed the subject, sublimity most commonly was associated with the awesome religious reverence that Milton evoked.[227] Richardson recommended that painters read the Holy Scriptures, for there they would find an inexhaustible spring of the most nobly expressed and most sublime thoughts.[228] Moving from verbal to pictorial example—from Milton to Raphael—Richardson applied critical notions gleaned from his literary experience to the art of painting and assured his readers that

> after having read *Milton,* one sees Nature with better Eyes than before, Beauties appear which else had been unregarded: So by conversing with the Works of the best Masters in Painting, one forms better Images whilst we are Reading, or Thinking. I see the Divine Airs of Raphael when I read any History of our Saviour; or the Blessed Virgin; and the Awful ones he gives an Apostle, when I read of their Actions that He, and Other great Men describe in a Nobler manner than otherwise I should ever have done.[229]

Noting that the term was not often applied to pictures, Richardson acknowledged that fewer painters than writers had attained the "sublime" and admitted that he had difficulty in precisely defining it for the visual arts. Nonetheless, the aspiration to sublimity might be likened to a search for the Holy Grail, an intangible goal toward which a painter must constantly aim. Richardson did not write of this, however, as an individualized quest so much as a national one. Though he conceded that the accomplishments of English painters had lagged behind their literary counterparts, he was confident that if ever the ancient, great, and beautiful taste in painting were revived, it would be in England. His optimism was spurred by his firm belief that England's Protestant faith made these artistic ambitions viable:

> Tis our Religion, which has open'd a New and a Noble Scene of Things; we have more Just and Enlarg'd Notions of the Deity, and more exalted ones of Humane Nature than the

225. *Saint Paul's Cathedral; a Poem,* London, 1750, 28–29.

226. This later eighteenth-century notion evolves from the distinction Edmund Burke made between the sublime and the beautiful (*A Philosophical Enquiry into the Origins of Our Ideas of the Sublime and Beautiful,* London, 1757); see A.F.B. Clark, *Boileau and the French Classical Critics in England, 1660–1830,* Geneva, (1925) 1978, 361.

227. Richardson was influenced by Boileau's French translation of Longinus, *Traité du Sublime où du Merveilleux dans le discours* (1674) which introduced thé treatise into the literary mainstream. Boileau's unpedantic and useful version was a deliberate departure from the original and came to be regarded as a "new" original; it was from Boileau's text that English translations were made (Pultney 1680; Welsted 1712). In its early usage, the sublime was not a quality of mind but an instrument of literary effect (J. Brody, *Boileau and Longinus,* Geneva, 1938, 37).

228. Richardson (1715) 1725, 201.

229. Ibid., 12. In the 1773 edition this passage was corrected grammatically; more interestingly, "or the Blessed Virgin" was deleted.

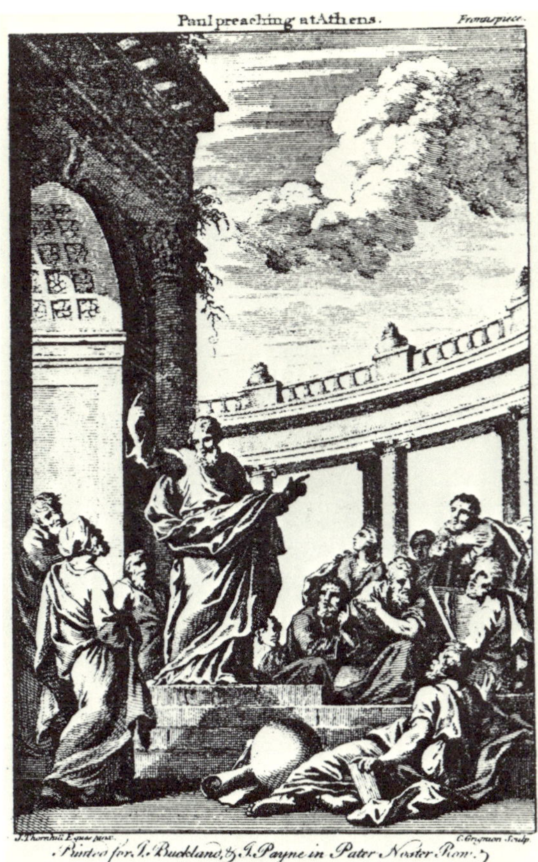

FIG. 74 James Thornhill, *Paul Preaching at Athens*, engraved by Charles Grignion, frontispiece to Thomas Gibbons, *Rhetoric*, 1767 (*cat. 30*)

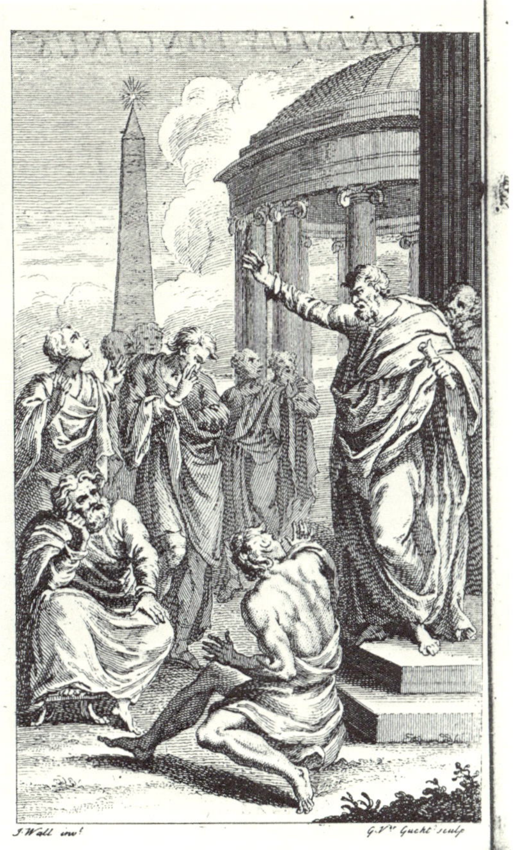

FIG. 75 *Paul Preaching at Athens*, engraved by Gerard Vandergucht (after J. Wall), frontispiece to Dionysus Longinus, *On the Sublime*, 1739 (*cat. 41*)

> Ancients could possibly have: And as there are some Fine Characters peculiar to the Christian Religion, it moreover affords some of the Noblest Subjects that ever were thought of for a Picture.[230]

BIBLE ILLUSTRATION, THORNHILL, AND THE PUBLISHING TRADE

Despite the widely acknowledged nobility of sacred themes, representations of religious subjects were still seen by some as a Jacobite threat to political stability. Still, the outcry was neither so menacing nor so strident as it had been in the early seventeenth century, when a long and venerable tradition of illustrating bibles was almost brought to a halt by Puritans who considered the inclusion of images a papist plot.[231] To answer the demands of those who welcomed illustrations as a devotional aid, some publishers bought prints abroad to bind into English bibles.[232] This practice of insertion increased and became considerably more public during the Restoration, although by the early eighteenth century some few bibles were published with plates that were locally produced.

230. Ibid., 224–26.

231. In the 1630s, even Bishop Laud did not dare openly to sanction illustrated bibles.

232. Regarding the practice of inserted plates which apparently spread from Scotland, and for an excellent overview of illustrations of the English Bible, see T. S. R. Boase, "Macklin and Bowyer," *Journal of the Warburg and Courtauld Institutes*, XXVI, 1963, 155–69.

In 1717 a whole new standard of illustration was set by a magnificent folio edition of the Bible published by John Baskett at Oxford. Thornhill produced some of the designs,[233] along with other artists whose engraving skills had been honed on the Acts of the Apostles: Claude Dubosc and Charles Dupuis, who had come to England to help Dorigny engrave the Cartoons (figs. 12, 16); Elisha Kirkall, who made a chiaroscuro woodcut after one of Giulio Romano's drawings after Raphael (fig. 14);[234] and Gerard Vandergucht, who engraved Thornhill's designs for the cupola of Saint Paul's (fig. 72). Other illustrated bibles of the period that were less virtuoso in performance often had illustrations described as "engraved from Designs of the Great Masters," which usually meant there were strong echoes of Raphael's Cartoons and Loggia frescos.[235] By 1755 the Cartoons themselves were used, albeit reengraved by Anthony Walker in an extremely small format, to illustrate *The New Testament . . . Adapted to the Capacities of Children.*

By mid-century, book publishers like Joseph Tonson who employed highly skilled engravers to render sacred as well as secular texts had substantially moved bible illustration out of the provincial realm and into the arena of sophisticated history painting. Thus, it was primarily through the medium of engraving that religious subjects joined the poetics of the sublime, as demonstrated by the frontispiece to the publication in 1739 of Longinus's treatise (fig. 75).[236] Thornhill was an early catalyst for this union, engaged as he was not only in large-scale history painting at Chatsworth and Greenwich and in English translations of Raphael at Saint Paul's, but also in smaller-scale works such as his illustrations for the Oxford and "Kitto" Bibles.[237]

Graphic depictions of pious subjects gained even greater cachet with the growing tide of Evangelicalism in the 1740s, when religious affections were kindled by the popular Methodist field preachers John Wesley and George Whitefield,[238] who by passionate pleading and winged imagination offered a respite from the dry, methodical, and unaffecting discourse of both Latitudinarian and Dissenting sermons.

THE RELIGIOUS PASSIONS AND THE SUBLIME

In this climate inclined towards sentiment and soul-searching, one can appreciate the new emotional appeal of several very large paintings executed in the 1740s for public display. A prime example is Hogarth's impassioned characterization of *Paul before Felix*, which he

233. Thornhill provided headpiece illustrations for Genesis, Leviticus, and Joshua and the tailpiece to Malachi, collaborating with Louis Chéron and Louis Laguerre.

234. With the aim of translating drawings into prints, Kirkall invented a new method of printing that combined etching, mezzotint, and woodblock. According to Walpole his chiaroscuro prints had much success and applause but no imitators, apparently because the method was too laborious and tedious (Walpole 1763, 120).

235. See, for example, the bible illustrations engraved by John Sturt and James Cole (Boase, "Macklin and Bowyer," 160–61).

236. The composition of the frontispiece to the most popular English edition of Longinus (*On the Sublime*, trans. by W. Smith, 1739) borrows ideas from Thornhill's painting *Paul Preaching at Athens* in the cupola of Saint Paul's and from Raphael's Cartoon of the same subject.

237. The "Kitto Bible"—sixty extra-illustrated volumes—contains a nearly complete set of small pen-and-wash designs by Thornhill that illustrate the New Testament (C. H. Collins-Baker, "Sir James Thornhill as Bible Illustrator," *Huntington Library Quarterly*, X, 1947, 323–27).

238. H. Davies, *Worship and Theology in England: from Watts and Wesley to Maurice, 1690–1850*, Princeton, 1961, 143–79.

painted for Lincoln's Inn in 1748. In the painted and two engraved versions (fig. 57),[239] Hogarth veers considerably from Raphael's chaste depiction of *Paul Preaching at Athens* (see fig. 7), a cartoon that he greatly admired and that basically served as his model. Similarly, a direct appeal to sentiment was made by the four large paintings executed for the Foundling Hospital by Hogarth, Francis Hayman, Joseph Highmore, and James Wills.[240] In their treatment of biblical stories, these works aim to move their audience—more pointedly, to elicit compassion or, as it was more commonly called, the "religious affections,"[241] which by 1746, the year these paintings were executed, were becoming a fashionable Christian response. The passions as presented in the Cartoons melded religious sentiment with the notion of sublimity and thus embraced the concerns of both philosophers and religious reformers. But with the rise of Evangelicalism in the 1740s, the passions were domesticated into an overt expression of sentiment.[242]

During the course of the next few decades, climaxing in the uncertainty and turmoil of the 1790s, the terms "passion" and "sublime" increasingly became associated with expressions of the subjective mind. Sublimity moved from the idea of nobility of mind to a darker vision—to the magnificent and dreadfully terrible. As the sublime found expression in visionary themes from Revelation, a taste for the forceful and fecund genius in Michelangelo's *Last Judgment* superseded appreciation for the magisterial calm of Raphael's apostles. Nevertheless, Raphael's work remained the core of academic teaching in England, despite Reynolds's ambivalent and tempered praise in his Academy lectures. And it is somewhat ironic that while Raphael continued to set the rules of art, Michelangelo—by transcending them—set the new standard of taste.

239. Another version was also executed in 1752, by Luke Sullivan.

240. Respectively, *Moses Brought before Pharaoh's Daughter*; *The Finding of Moses*; *Hagar and Ishmael*; *Little Children Brought to Christ*.

241. The various senses of the word "passion" and its relationship to the word "affection," which was used to denote a more gentle response, is described by I. Watts in *The Doctrine of the Passions explained and improved, or a brief comprehensive scheme of the natural affections*, London, 1739.

242. W. R. Ward, "The Eighteenth-Century Church: A European View," in Walsh, 290.

VI. RAPHAEL REVISED AT THE ACADEMY

THE PENDULUM SWUNG slightly in the other direction when Reynolds died in 1792 and Benjamin West took up the presidency of the Royal Academy. Although West had settled in England in 1763 and never returned to America, the sobriquet the "American Raphael" still clung from his early reputation as a promising young painter in Rome when he was under the wings of the classicizing Anton Raphael Mengs and the influential Cardinal Albani. West's reverence for Raphael continued through the years he headed the Academy,[243] and Thomas Lawrence's *Portrait of Benjamin West* (see fig. 76)[244] showing him beside his own copy of Raphael's *Death of Ananias* seems a pointed riposte to the Reynolds's memorial in Saint Paul's—a statue that states his artistic allegiance with a portrait of Michelangelo carved on its plinth.

Under West's direction the Cartoons were engraved anew in 1800, this time by three *English* artists, Thomas Holloway and his pupils Robert Slann and Thomas S. Webb.[245] The impetus for this large folio volume of prints—a more tonal translation than Dorigny's hard linear style—may have been the arrival that year of the duke of Bedford's gift of Thornhill's full-size copies to the Royal Academy (see fig. 24).[246] Four years later, when their removal from the exhibition gallery at Somerset House was being discussed, West was especially keen to keep Thornhill's copies on exhibit. He argued from a new perspective that the arrangement of the color in the Cartoons was as masterly as their compositions, and that this could not be known from the prints.[247]

Raphael's *Death of Ananias* was the centerpiece of West's last lecture to the Academy in 1817, on the subject of the immutability of the colors of the rainbow.[248] West's lecture was originally scheduled for 1816, when the original Cartoon had been lent to the Academy for students to copy,[249] but ill health forced its postponement. By the time the lecture was delivered, the original had been returned, and Thornhill's full-size copy apparently was no longer hanging. In need of a demonstration piece, West undoubtedly made use of the off-tract by Dorigny, which he himself had painted over in oils.[250] It seems particularly fitting

243. For a summary of West's various visits to see the Cartoons, see S. Dickey, "Raphael's Tapestry Cartoons for the Sistine Chapel and British Painting of the Later Eighteenth Century," M.A. thesis, New York University Institute of Fine Arts, 1980, 9 and n. 26. She focuses primarily on the influence of the Cartoons as formal models.

244. Commissioned in 1818 for the American Academy of Fine Art of New York, the portrait was completed in 1820–21 and sold to the Wadsworth Atheneum, Hartford, in 1855. A replica in the Tate Gallery was painted for George IV in 1836. Exhibited here is the engraving executed by Charles Rolls in 1842.

245. The last plate was not completed until 1830, two years after Holloway died.

246. They arrived at the Academy on 11 May 1800 (Farington, IV, 1394).

247. Ibid., VI, 2274 (24 March 1804). The copies were probably removed sometime in 1804, but under the urging of West and Fuseli they were reinstalled on 11 February 1805 (VII, 2510, 2513, 2515).

248. D. A. Brown, *Raphael in America*, Washington, DC, 1983, 17.

249. Farington, XIV, 4942–3 (13 December 1816).

250. Benjamin West's sons put up a set of copies of the Cartoons for auction in 1820 (Christies, London, 23–24 June) and again in 1829 (Geo. Robins, London, 20 and 22 June). Five of them allegedly were colored by Thornhill upon the original off-tracts used by Dorigny for his plates and the remaining two, *The Death of Ananias* and *Christ's Charge to Peter*, were colored by West (one is signed and dated 1785, location unknown; see H. von Erffa and A. Staley, *The Paintings of Benjamin West*, New Haven, 1986, cat. no. 513). The 1829 sale also included the painting by West, presumably shown in Lawrence's portrait behind the easel, "The curious picture of the two prismatic spheres, illustrative of the System of Col-

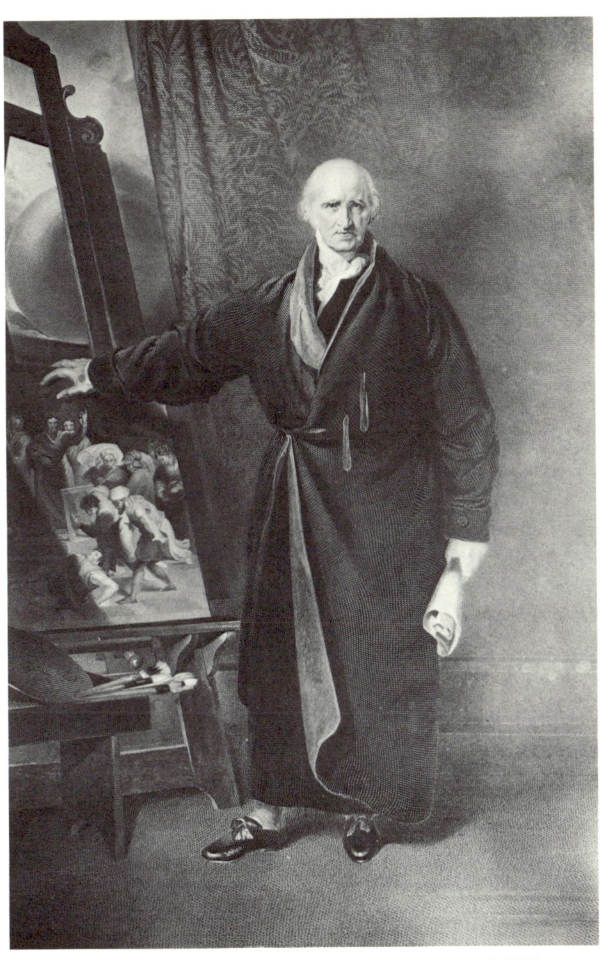

FIG. 76 Thomas Lawrence, *Portrait of Benjamin West* (1820), engraved by Charles Rolls, 1842 (*cat. 16*)

that this final tribute to Raphael became part of his own commemorative portrait by Lawrence.

West's basic idea was that the arrangement of colors in historical painting ought to conform to the order of the colors in the rainbow–the warm and brilliant colors confined to where the principal light falls and the cool colors to the shade.[251] This he believed could best be demonstrated in the Cartoons, but he remarked that in the Vatican Stanze Raphael had not followed this principle.[251] Joseph Farington recounts a conversation with West apropos of his lecture:

> West said, that the progress made in acquiring knowledge of the Science of Colouring occupied several Centuries, and was attained in perfection by *Raphael*, as shown in the Cartoons, which West considered as being the most perfect examples of arrangement of Colours in the World; *tones*, they could not have, as the Cartoons does not admit of it, but the Harmony of colours, as far as arrangement goes, is as perfect as the prism, and the principles upon which Raphael made his arrangement as true as any of the established discoveries of Sir Isaac Newton.[252]

Just as Richardson a century earlier had found Raphael's' performance in the Vatican not up to the measure of Hampton Court, West also found that the paintings in the Stanze did not conform so perfectly to the principles of true harmonious color arrangement as did the Cartoons. He earlier remarked that Raphael's deft arrangement of groups and his expert disposition of light and shade to produce the general effect were not sufficiently appreciated.[253] With great ingenuity, Raphael's late eighteenth-century defenders gained points for

ouring, and referred to by the Professor of Painting to the Royal Academy."

Three sets of engravings by Dorigny were listed in Thornhill Sale B (26 February, Portfolio C, 13, 19, and Portfolio D, 9) but with no mention that any were colored by him. Indeed, the colored off-tracts in the West sale may well have been by Goupy, who frequently painted in gouache over engravings. See above pp. 41–42 and n. 117, and von Erffa and Staley.

251. Farington, XIV, 5120–21 (4 December 1817).

252. Ibid., 4944 (14 December 1816).

253. Ibid., XI, 4140 (7 June 1812). In this respect it appears that West wanted to reclaim for Raphael what De Piles had claimed for Rubens a century earlier: prowess in managing the "general effect," then termed the *toute ensemble* (T. Puttfarken, *Roger de Piles' Theory of Art*, New Haven, 1985, 54–55).

him that even Richardson had not scored.[254] It seems there was scarcely a formal element in the whole art of painting for which the Cartoons did not offer an exemplary answer. The praises of Raphael sung in Reynolds's early *Discourses* echo through the lectures of succeeding Royal Academicians, including West, Henry Fuseli, Joseph M. W. Turner, John Opie, and James Barry.[255]

During West's tenure as president of the Royal Academy, Turner, as professor of perspective, regularly lectured in the Great Room at Somerset House, where Thornhill's full-size copies of Raphael were hung. Like West, Turner frequently referred to the Cartoons, but he now looked to the underlying geometry of their composition, claiming that "the lines . . . as lines never had a line of praise."[256] He particularly noted Raphael's success in exploring the effects of parallel perspective to obtain grandeur in *Paul Preaching at Athens,*

> where perspective introductions were essential to the subject, and by means of the high horizon and the steps, only Paul possesses that elevation which, together with the simple yet energetic form, commands that attention by situation, and which the nature of the subject demanded. And if we were to divest the lines of light, shade and colour, Paul would hold the same power of elevation by lines only.[257]

Turner's small sketch of Paul which reduces the figure to a linear scaffold (fig. 77)[258] is a reminder that the Cartoons accommodated his ideas on perspective as readily as Hogarth's notions of delineating character. But while artists and connoisseurs summoned Raphael's authority to validate their own ideas, a wider audience also laid claim to the Acts of the Apostles.

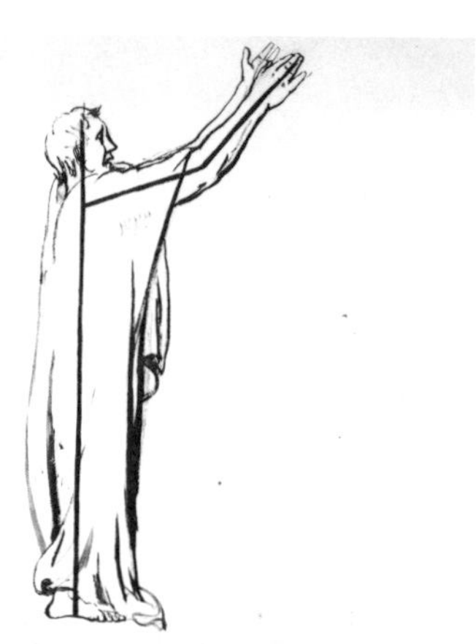

FIG. 77 Joseph Mallord William Turner, *Paul Preaching,* ca.1812, pen and ink, Tate Gallery, London

A critical factor in the influential role of the Hampton Court Cartoons (and their many replications) was that they embraced the values of both the Apostolic and the Augustan Age. In these paintings, Georgian England saw the foundations of its Protestant faith described in perfect accordance with the precepts of its classical education. The New Kingdom heralded by the historic apostles in the first century thus had an eighteenth-century counterpart in the United Kingdom, where Raphael's apostles were naturalized and became the heralds of England's artistic coming of age.

254. Richardson 1773, 190, recommends an eighteen-point rating system for composition, design, coloring, and expression which derives from de Piles, *Cours de Peinture,* see n. 185.

255. See R. Wornum, *Lectures on Painting by the Royal Academicians Barry, Opie, and Fuseli,* London, 1848, for repeated references to Raphael.

256. British Museum, Add. MSS. 46,151, K, f.211. References to the Cartoons are dotted throughout Turner's lecture notes, MMS. 46, 151, A, f.14v; C, f.17r; M, f.1v.

257. J. Ziff, "'Backgrounds: Introduction of Architecture and Landscape,' A Lecture by J. M. W. Turner," *Journal of the Warburg and Courtauld Institutes,* XXVI, 1963, 134.

258. M. Davies, *Turner as Professor: The Artist and Linear Perspective,* London, 1992, 54–55, 108, and n. 104. The sketch is on paper with an 1812 watermark and was probably used sometime after that date to illustrate one of his lectures.

WORKS IN THE EXHIBITION

GERARD AUDRAN

1. *The Death of Ananias* (after Charles Jervas, after Raphael), ca.1702-3
engraving and etching, 23 x 27½ in.
Board of Trustees of the Victoria and Albert Museum, London
(fig. 18)

WILLIAM JAMES BENNETT

2. *View of the Hampton Court Gallery*, in William H. Pyne, *History of the Royal Residences*, vol. 2, London, 1819
color aquatint, after J. Stephenoff
Print Collection, Miriam and Ira D. Wallach Division of Art, Prints and Photographs, The New York Public Library, Astor, Lenox and Tilden Foundations
(fig. 9)

JOHN BURNET

3. *The Death of Ananias* (after Raphael), 1837
etching on steel, 17¾ x 28$\frac{3}{16}$ in.
The Metropolitan Museum of Art, A. Hyatt Mayor Purchase Fund, Marjorie Phelps Starr Bequest, 1982

NICOLAS DORIGNY

4. *Pinacotheca Hamptoniana*, London, 1719
Yale Center for British Art, Paul Mellon Collection

Set of seven engravings after Raphael's Tapestry Cartoons (*Pinacotheca Hamptoniana*, 1719)
20½ x 24½ in. and 20½ x 29½ in.
Board of Trustees of the Victoria and Albert Museum, London

4a. *The Miraculous Draught of Fishes*

4b. *Christ's Charge to Peter*

4c. *The Lame Man Healed* (fig. 12; detail, fig. 31)

4d. *The Death of Ananias*

4e. *Elymas the Sorcerer Struck with Blindness*

4f. *Paul and Barnabas at Lystra* (detail, fig. 21)

4g. *Paul Preaching at Athens* (fig. 16)

R. DUPPA

5. *Heads from the Fresco Pictures of Raffaello in the Vatican*, London, 1802
Art and Architecture Collection, Miriam and Ira D. Wallach Division of Art, Prints and Photographs, The New York Public Library, Astor, Lenox and Tilden Foundations
(fig. 70)

GIOVANNI BATTISTA FRANCO

6. *The Lame Man Healed* (after Raphael), mid-16th century
engraving, 9⅞ x 16 in.
The Metropolitan Museum of Art, Harris Brisbane Dick Fund, 1926
(fig. 13)

GIORGIO GHISI

7. *School of Athens* (after Raphael), 1550
engraving, 20¼ x 31$\frac{15}{16}$ in.
The Metropolitan Museum of Art, Harris Brisbane Dick Fund, 1925
(fig. 34)

SIMON GRIBELIN

8. *The Tent of Darius* (after Charles Le Brun), 1693 in André Félibien, *The Tent of Darius Explain'd: or the Queens of Persia at the Feet of Alexander*, trans. Col. Parsons, London, 1703 (this copy with annotations by Sir Joshua Reynolds)
Art and Architecture Collection, Miriam and Ira D. Wallach Division of Art, Prints and Photographs, Research Libraries, The New York Public Library, Astor, Lenox and Tilden Foundations
(fig. 45)

Set of seven engravings after Raphael's Tapestry Cartoons (1707) 1720, and *A View of the Hampton Court Cartoon Gallery*, 1720
each 7¼ x 8½ in.
Museum of Fine Arts, Boston, Harvey D. Parker Collection, 1897

9. *A View of the Hampton Court Cartoon Gallery* (fig. 8)

9a. *The Miraculous Draught of Fishes*

9b. *Christ's Charge to Peter*

9c. *The Lame Man Healed* (fig. 11)

9d. *The Death of Ananias*

9e. *Elymas the Sorcerer Struck with Blindness*

9f. *Paul and Barnabas at Lystra* (detail, fig. 20)

9g. *Paul Preaching at Athens* (fig. 15)

WILLIAM HOGARTH

10. *Characters and Caricaturas*, 1743
engraving and etching, 10¾ x 8⅞ in.
The Metropolitan Museum of Art,
Harris Brisbane Dick Fund, 1932
(figs. 58, 58a)

11. *Paul before Felix*, 1752
engraving and etching, 16⅝ x 20⅝ in.
The Metropolitan Museum of Art,
Harris Brisbane Dick Fund, 1932
(fig. 57)

12. *Analysis of Beauty*, London, 1753
Avery Architectural and Fine Arts Library,
Columbia University in the City of New York

12a. *Statuary Yard*, 1753, plate 1 in *Analysis of Beauty*
engraving and etching, 14½ x 19⅜ in.
The Metropolitan Museum of Art,
Harris Brisbane Dick Fund, 1932
(figs. 56, 56a)

13. *The Bench*, 1st state, 1758
engraving and etching, 8 x 6½ in.
Museum of Fine Arts, Boston,
Harvey D. Parker Collection, 1897
(fig. 61)

13a. *The Bench*, 5th state (1758), 1764
engraving and etching, 8 x 6½ in.
Courtesy of the Print Collection, The Lewis Walpole Library, Yale University
(fig. 61a)

14. *Heads of Elymas and Three Men* (after Raphael), 1781
engraving and etching, 8½ x 14 in.
The Metropolitan Museum of Art,
Harris Brisbane Dick Fund, 1932
(fig. 64)

ELISHA KIRKALL

15. *Disputation in the Temple* (after Giulio Romano, after Raphael), 1722
mezzotint and wood block, 17¼ x 23 in.
Board of Trustees of the Victoria and Albert Museum, London
(fig. 14)

THOMAS LAWRENCE

16. *Portrait of Benjamin West* (1820)
engraved by Charles Rolls, 1842, 23¾ x 15⅝ in.
Courtesy, American Antiquarian Society, Worcester, Massachusetts
(fig. 76)

CHARLES LE BRUN (after)

17. *Expressions des Passions de l'Ame*, engraved by Martin Engelbrecht, Augsburg, 1732
The Metropolitan Museum of Art,
Harris Brisbane Dick Fund, 1953

17a. *A Method to Learn to Design the Passions, Proposed in a Conference on the General and Particular Expression*, engraved by John Williams, London, 1734
Yale Center for British Art,
Paul Mellon Collection

17b. Title page to *Heads Representing the Various Passions of the Soul*, London, mid-18th century
engraving, 14⅜ x 9¼ in.
The Metropolitan Museum of Art,
The Elisha Whittelsey Collection,
The Elisha Whittelsey Fund, 1953
(fig. 46)

17c. *Anger*, in *Heads Representing the Various Passions of the Soul*, mid-18th century
engraving, 14¼ x 10⅛ in.
The Metropolitan Museum of Art,
The Elisha Whittelsey Collection,
The Elisha Whittelsey Fund, 1953
(fig. 48)

NICOLAS LE SUEUR

18. *Christ's Charge to Peter* (after Raphael), from *Cabinet de Crozat*, vol. 1, Paris, 1729

chiaroscuro wood engraving, 10⅛ x 14⅜ in.
The Metropolitan Museum of Art,
Gift of Harry G. Friedman, 1960
(fig. 22)

ANTON RAPHAEL MENGS

19. *Le LII Teste della Celebre Scuola d'Atene Dipinta da Raffaello Sanzio da Urbino nel Palazzo Vaticano Desegnate in XL Carte dal Cavalier Anton Raphael Mengs*, engraved by Domenico Cunego, Rome, 1785
National Gallery of Art Library
(fig. 67)

ARTHUR POND and CHARLES KNAPTON

20. *Paul Preaching at Athens* (after Panini), from *Prints in Imitation of Drawings*, London, 1736
engraving, 7⅝ x 10¼ in.
The Metropolitan Museum of Art,
Harris Brisbane Dick Fund, 1923
(fig. 23)

21. *Woman with a Water Jug* (after Raphael), from *Prints in Imitation of Drawings*, London, 1736
engraving, 16¼ x 7⅝ in.
The Metropolitan Museum of Art,
Harris Brisbane Dick Fund, 1923

MARCANTONIO RAIMONDI

22. *Parnassus* (after Raphael), ca.1517-20
engraving, 14 x 18½ in.
The Metropolitan Museum of Art,
Bequest of James Clark McGuire, 1931
(fig. 17)

BENJAMIN RALPH

23. *School of Raphael, or the Student's Guide to Expression in Historical Painting*, London, 1759
Yale Center for British Art,
Paul Mellon Collection
(fig. 35)

23a. *School of Raphael, or the Student's Guide to Expression in Historical Painting*, London, 1825
Avery Architectural and Fine Arts Library,
Columbia University in the City of New York
(fig. 36)

23b. *A New Drawing Book of Heads, from the Cartoons at Hampton Court*, London, 18th century
Yale Center for British Art,
Paul Mellon Collection

RAPHAEL (after)

24. *The Death of Ananias*, ca.1685
wool and silk tapestry, woven at Mortlake,
12 ft. 4 in. x 19 ft.
The Cathedral Church of St. John the Divine,
Gift of Mary Louise Brugière
(fig. 10)

JONATHAN RICHARDSON SR. and JR.

25. *An Account of Some of the Statues, Bas-Reliefs, Drawings, and Pictures in Italy, &c., with Remarks*, London, 1722
Avery Architectural and Fine Arts Library,
Columbia University in the City of New York

THOMAS ROWLANDSON

26. A set of nineteen etchings from *Le Brun Travested or Caricatures of the Passions*, London, 1800, designed by George M. Woodward and etched by Thomas Rowlandson
hand-colored etchings, each 10⅝ x 8¾ in.
Courtesy of the Print Collection, The Lewis Walpole Library, Yale University

26a. Attention

26b. Admiration

26c. Admiration with Astonishment

26d. Veneration (fig. 55)

26e. Rapture

26f. Desire

26g. Joy with Tranquillity

26h. Laughter (fig. 54)

26i. Acute Pain

26j. Simple Bodily Pain

26k. Sadness

26l. Weeping

26m. Compassion (fig. 53)

26n. Scorn

26o. Horror

26p. Terror or Fright

26q. Anger (fig. 49)

26r. Hatred or Jealousy

26s. Despair

GEORGE SCHARF

27. *Lecture on Sculpture by Sir Richard Westmacott, at the Royal Academy, Somerset House, 1830*, 1836
lithograph, 7¾ x 12⅜ in.
Guildhall Library, Corporation of London
(fig. 24)

JAMES THORNHILL

28. *Paul before Agrippa*, ca.1710
oil on canvas, 32¼ x 29¼ in.
Yale Center for British Art,
Paul Mellon Collection
(fig. 71)

29. Set of eight engravings after Thornhill's designs for the Cupola of Saint Paul's Cathedral, London, ca.1720
each 16 x 10½ in.
Cooper-Hewitt, National Design Museum,
Smithsonian Institution,
Gift of William R. Osmun, 1952

29a. *Conversion of Paul*, engraved by Claude Dubosc

29b. *Paul and Barnabas Preaching in a City by Lycaonia*, engraved by Bernard Baron

29c. *Paul before King Agrippa*, engraved by Charles-Louis Simonneau (fig. 73)

29d. *Paul on Melita Strikes the Venomous Serpent from Him into the Fire*,
engraved by Gerard Vandergucht

29e. *Paul and Silas in Prison Comforting Their Keeper*, engraved by Gerard Vandergucht

29f. *Paul Preaching at Athens*,
engraved by Gerard Vandergucht (fig. 72)

29g. *Paul Oversees Converted Greeks Who Burn Books of Necromancy*, engraved by Gerard Vandergucht

29h. *Paul Stricken Blind before the Prophets of Antioch*, engraved by Nicolas-Dauphin Beauvais

30. *Paul Preaching at Athens*, engraved by Charles Grignion, frontispiece to
Thomas Gibbons, *Rhetoric; or, a View of Its Principal Tropes and Figures, in Their Origin and Powers*, London (1767), reprint 1969
Butler Library, Columbia University Libraries
(fig. 74)

31. Album of 162 small drawings after Raphael's Tapestry Cartoons, ca.1729–31
pen, brown ink, and wash,
each drawing approx. 4½ x 6¾ in.
Board of Trustees of the Victoria and Albert Museum, London
(figs. 29, 37-44, 60, 62)

Set of seven oil paintings after Raphael's Tapestry Cartoons, ca.1729-31
Columbia University of the City of New York,
Gift of Mrs. Francis Henry Lenygon, 1959

32. *The Miraculous Draught of Fishes*, 67½ x 81⅝ in. (fig. 1)

33. *Christ's Charge to Peter*, 66½ x 86¾ in. (fig. 2)

34. *The Lame Man Healed*, 66½ x 107 in. (fig. 3)

35. *The Death of Ananias*, 66¾ x 103¾ in. (fig. 4)

36. *Elymas the Sorcerer Struck with Blindness*, 66⅝ x 86⅞ in. (fig. 5)

37. *Paul and Barnabas at Lystra*, 67¼ x 107¼ in. (fig. 6)

38. *Paul Preaching at Athens*, 66¼ x 86¼ in. (fig. 7)

39. *Study for a Group Portrait of the Artist and His Family*, ca.1730
pen, brown ink, and wash, 8¾ x 19¾ in.
Burghley House Collection
(fig. 25)

40. *A Niche for Mr. Portman's House at Sherborne*
pen, brown ink, and wash, $9\frac{13}{16}$ x 10⅛ in.
Yale Center for British Art,
Paul Mellon Collection
(fig. 33)

GERARD VANDERGUCHT

41. *Paul Preaching at Athens* (after J. Wall), frontispiece to Dionysus Longinus, *On the Sublime*, trans. William Smith, London, 1739.
Courtesy of the Division of Rare and Manuscript Collections, Cornell University Library
(fig. 75)

FREQUENTLY CITED SOURCES

CROFT-MURRAY

Edward Croft-Murray, *Decorative Painting in England, 1537–1837,* 2 vols., London, 1962.

FARINGTON

Joseph Farington, *Diary of Joseph Farington,* 16 vols., New Haven, 1978–84.

GIBSON-WOOD 1982

Carol Gibson-Wood, "Studies in the Theory of Connoisseurship from Vasari to Morelli," Ph.D. diss., University of London, 1982.

GIBSON-WOOD 1984

Carol Gibson-Wood, "Jonathan Richardson and the Rationalization of Connoisseurship," *Art History,* VII, March 1984, 38–56.

GIBSON-WOOD 1993

Carol Gibson-Wood, "The Political Background to Thornhill's Paintings in St. Paul's Cathedral," *Journal of the Warbury Courtauld Institutes,* LVI, 1993, 229–37.

MARILLIER MS. NOTES

H. C. Marillier, manuscript notes in the subject catalogue, Department of Textiles, Victoria and Albert Museum.

MARILLIER 1962

H. C. Marillier, *The Tapestries at Hampton Court,* London, 1962.

MORRIS

David B. Morris, *The Religious Sublime: Christian Poetry and Critical Tradition in Eighteenth-Century England,* Louisville, KY, 1972.

PAULSON

Ronald Paulson, *Hogarth: Art and Politics, 1750–1764,* New Brunswick, NJ, 1993.

REYNOLDS

Joshua Reynolds, *Discourses on Art (1797),* ed. Robert R. Walk, New Haven, 1975.

RICHARDSON (1715) 1725

Jonathan Richardson Sr., *An Essay on the Theory of Painting,* London (1715), 1725.

RICHARDSON 1722

Jonathan Richardson Sr. and Jr., *An Account of Some of the Statues, Bas-Reliefs, Drawings, and Pictures in Italy, &c., with Remarks,* London, 1722.

RICHARDSON 1773

Jonathan Richardson Sr., *The Works of Jonathan Richardson,* London, 1773 (includes "An Essay on the Theory of Painting" [1715]; "An Essay on the Art of Criticism, &c." [1719]; "A Discourse on the Dignity, Certainty, Pleasure and Advantage of the Science of a Connoisseur" [1719]).

RICHARDSON 1792

Jonathan Richardson Sr., *The Works of Jonathan Richardson,* London, 1792 (with additions of "An Essay on the Knowledge of Prints," and "Cautions to Collectors").

ROSENBERG 1979

Martin I. Rosenberg, "Raphael in French Art Theory, Criticism, and Practice, 1660–1830," Ph.D. diss., University of Pennsylvania, 1979.

ROSENBERG 1995

Martin I. Rosenberg, *Raphael and France*, University Park, PA, 1995.

RUPP

Gordon Rupp, *Religion in England, 1688–1791*, Oxford, 1986.

THORNHILL SALE A

A catalogue of the intire collection belonging to Sir James Thornhill, late Principal History Painter to His Majesty, &c., consistisng of several very capital pictures, 24–25 February 1734/5 (Lugt 433; reprinted in "Editorial: Sir James Thornhill's Collection," *Burlington Magazine*, June 1943, 133–36).

THORNHILL SALE B

A catalogue of the collection of prints, drawings, and casts belonging to Sir James Thornhill, 26–28 February 1734/5 (not in Lugt).

VERTUE I

The Notebooks of George Vertue, *Walpole Society: Vertue I*, XVIII, 1930. (A wide selection of George Vertue's notebooks in the British Museum was published by the *Walpole Society: Vertue I–VI*, 1929–50. These manuscripts, a chronicle of English art that he began in 1712, are the basis of Horace Walpole's *Anecdotes on Painting in England*, 4 vols., London, 1762–71).

VERTUE III

The Notebooks of George Vertue, *Walpole Society: Vertue III*, XXII, 1934.

VERTUE IV

The Notebooks of George Vertue, *Walpole Society: Vertue IV*, XXIV, 1936.

VERTUE MSS.

Unpublished Vertue manuscripts, British Museum, MSS. 23,081, f.89–90; also in Gibson-Wood 1982, 261–76 (Appendix IV: Some upublished notes by George Vertue on the writings of Jonathan Richardson).

WALPOLE 1763

Horace Walpole, *A Catalogue of Engravers who have been born or resided in England*, London, 1763.

WALPOLE IV

Horace Walpole, *Anecdotes of Painting in England*, London, vol.4, 1771 (see note to Vertue I above).

WALSH

John Walsh, Colin Haydon, Stephen Taylor, eds., *The Church of England c.1689–c.1833: From Toleration to Tractarianism*, Cambridge, 1993.

WHITLEY

William Thomas Whitley, *Artists and Their Friends in England, 1700–1799* (1928), 2 vols., London, 1968.

This catalogue has been set in Baskerville and Bell types
and printed on Mohawk Superfine, Mohawk Vellum, and Karma Natural paper
at The Stinehour Press in Lunenburg, Vermont.
Designed by Jerry Kelly.